L.M. Montgomery

**ALSO IN THE
EXTRAORDINARY CANADIANS
SERIES:**

Big Bear by Rudy Wiebe

Lord Beaverbrook by David Adams Richards

Norman Bethune by Adrienne Clarkson

Emily Carr by Lewis DeSoto

Tommy Douglas by Vincent Lam

Glenn Gould by Mark Kingwell

Louis-Hippolyte LaFontaine and Robert Baldwin
by John Ralston Saul

Wilfrid Laurier by André Pratte

Stephen Leacock by Margaret MacMillan

René Lévesque by Daniel Poliquin

Nellie McClung by Charlotte Gray

Marshall McLuhan by Douglas Coupland

Lester B. Pearson by Andrew Cohen

Maurice Richard by Charles Foran

Mordecai Richler by M.G. Vassanji

Louis Riel and Gabriel Dumont by Joseph Boyden

Pierre Elliott Trudeau by Nino Ricci

SERIES EDITOR:
John Ralston Saul

L.M. Montgomery
by JANE URQUHART

With an Introduction by
John Ralston Saul
SERIES EDITOR

EXTRAORDINARY
CANADIANS

PENGUIN CANADA

Published by the Penguin Group

Penguin Group (Canada), 90 Eglinton Avenue East, Suite 700,
Toronto, Ontario, Canada M4P 2Y3 (a division of Pearson Canada Inc.)

Penguin Group (USA) Inc., 375 Hudson Street, New York, New York 10014, U.S.A.
Penguin Books Ltd, 80 Strand, London WC2R 0RL, England
Penguin Ireland, 25 St Stephen's Green, Dublin 2, Ireland
(a division of Penguin Books Ltd)
Penguin Group (Australia), 250 Camberwell Road, Camberwell, Victoria 3124, Australia
(a division of Pearson Australia Group Pty Ltd)
Penguin Books India Pvt Ltd, 11 Community Centre, Panchsheel Park,
New Delhi – 110 017, India
Penguin Group (NZ), 67 Apollo Drive, Rosedale, North Shore 0745, Auckland,
New Zealand (a division of Pearson New Zealand Ltd)
Penguin Books (South Africa) (Pty) Ltd, 24 Sturdee Avenue, Rosebank,
Johannesburg 2196, South Africa

Penguin Books Ltd, Registered Offices: 80 Strand, London WC2R 0RL, England

First published 2009

1 2 3 4 5 6 7 8 9 10 (RRD)

Copyright © Jane Urquhart, 2009
Introduction copyright © John Ralston Saul, 2009

Quotations from *The Selected Journals of L.M. Montgomery, Volumes 1–5*, edited by Mario
Rubio and Elizabeth Waterston are reprinted by permission of Oxford University Press.
Copyright © University of Guelph 1985.

L.M. Montgomery is a trademark of Heirs of L.M. Montgomery Inc.

Manufactured in the U.S.A.

LIBRARY AND ARCHIVES CANADA CATALOGUING IN PUBLICATION

Urquhart, Jane, 1949–
Lucy Maud Montgomery / Jane Urquhart.

(Extraordinary Canadians)
Includes bibliographical references.
ISBN 978-0-670-06675-9

1. Montgomery, L. M. (Lucy Maud), 1874–1942.
1. Montgomery, L. M. (Lucy Maud), 1874–1942.
I. Title. II. Series: Extraordinary Canadians
PS8526.O55Z92 2009   C813'.52   C2009-902416-0

Visit the Penguin Group (Canada) website at **www.penguin.ca**

Special and corporate bulk purchase rates available; please see
www.penguin.ca/corporatesales or call 1-800-810-3104, ext. 477 or 474

This book was printed on 30% PCW recycled paper

To Elizabeth Waterston and Mary Rubio
from a grateful student

CONTENTS

Introduction by John Ralston Saul   IX

1   Her Death   I

2   Orphan   II

3   Love   21

4   In a Man's World   41

5   Sorrow   61

6   Places   81

7   The Work   95

8   Madness   III

9   Sleep   133

10   Her Reader   141

SOURCES   151

ACKNOWLEDGMENTS   155

CHRONOLOGY   157

John Ralston Saul

How do civilizations imagine themselves? One way is for each of us to look at ourselves through our society's most remarkable figures. I'm not talking about hero worship or political iconography. That is a danger to be avoided at all costs. And yet people in every country do keep on going back to the most important people in their past.

This series of Extraordinary Canadians brings together rebels, reformers, martyrs, writers, painters, thinkers, political leaders. Why? What is it that makes them relevant to us so long after their deaths?

For one thing, their contributions are there before us, like the building blocks of our society. More important than that are their convictions and drive, their sense of what is right and wrong, their willingness to risk all, whether it be their lives, their reputations, or simply being wrong in public. Their ideas, their triumphs and failures, all of these somehow constitute a mirror of our society. We look at these people, all dead, and discover what we have been, but also what we can be. A mirror is an instrument for measuring ourselves. What we see can be both a warning and an encouragement.

These eighteen biographies of twenty key Canadians are centred on the meaning of each of their lives. Each of them is very different, but these are not randomly chosen great figures. Together they produce a grand sweep of the creation of modern Canada, from our first steps as a democracy in 1848 to our questioning of modernity late in the twentieth century.

All of them except one were highly visible on the cutting edge of their day while still in their twenties, thirties, and forties. They were young, driven, curious. An astonishing level of fresh energy surrounded them and still does. We in the twenty-first century talk endlessly of youth, but power today is often controlled by people who fear the sort of risks and innovations embraced by everyone in this series. A number of them were dead—hanged, infected on a battlefield, broken by their exertions—well before middle age. Others hung on into old age, often profoundly dissatisfied with themselves.

Each one of these people has changed you. In some cases you know this already. In others you will discover how through these portraits. They changed the way the world hears music, thinks of war, communicates. They changed how each of us sees what surrounds us, how minorities are treated, how we think of immigrants, how we look after each other, how we imagine ourselves through what are now our stories.

You will notice that many of them were people of the word. Not just the writers. Why? Because civilizations are built around many themes, but they require a shared public language. So Laurier, Bethune, Douglas, Riel, LaFontaine, McClung, Trudeau, Lévesque, Big Bear, even Carr and Gould, were masters of the power of language. Beaverbrook was one of the most powerful newspaper publishers of his day. Countries need action and laws and courage. But civilization is not a collection of prime ministers. Words, words, words—it is around these that civilizations create and imagine themselves.

The authors I have chosen for each subject are not the obvious experts. They are imaginative, questioning minds from among our leading writers and activists. They have, each one of them, a powerful connection to their subject. And in their own lives, each is engaged in building what Canada is now becoming.

That is why a documentary is being filmed around each subject. Images are yet another way to get at each subject and to understand their effect on us.

The one continuous, essential voice of biography since 1961 has been the *Dictionary of Canadian Biography*. But there has not been a project of book-length biographies such as Extraordinary Canadians in a hundred years, not since the Makers of Canada series. And yet every generation understands the past differently, and so sees in the mirror of these remarkable figures somewhat different lessons. As history rolls on, some truths remain the same while others are revealed in a new and unexpected way.

What strikes me again and again is just how dramatically ethical decisions figured in these people's lives. They form the backbone of history and memory. Some of them, Big Bear, for example, or Dumont, or even Lucy Maud Montgomery, thought of themselves as failures by the end of their lives. But the ethical cord that was strung taut through their work has now carried them on to a new meaning and even greater strength, long after their deaths.

Each of these stories is a revelation of the tough choices unusual people must make to find their way. And each of us as readers will find in the desperation of the Chinese revolution, the search for truth in fiction, the political and military dramas, different meanings that strike a personal chord. At first it is that personal emotive link to such figures which draws us in. Then we find they are a key that opens the whole society of their time to us. Then we realize that in that 150-year period many of them knew each other, were friends, opposed each other. Finally, when all these stories are put together, you will see that a whole new debate has been created around Canadian civilization and the shape of our continuous experiment.

Early feminism came in many forms. Nellie McClung led in creating the language and the political structure for the movement. Emily Carr's stubborn brilliance remade the image all Canadians have of themselves and their place.

But Lucy Maud Montgomery was the most complex of the famous women of that era. In her novels she puts forward the world almost as it should be, and this world somehow speaks to people across borders and across time. In her public, middle-class life, she hid behind the rigid disguise of an Edwardian matron of the most formidable sort. And then, in her diaries—clearly written to become her public testament—she reveals her full suffering and the strength that a brilliant and driven woman needed to make her way.

Only a remarkable novelist like Jane Urquhart could separate out these three people who made up Lucy Maud Montgomery. She separates them and puts them back together in order to make sense of the woman, the writer, and the leader who, in her own tortured way, pointed toward a different sort of womanhood.

CHAPTER ONE

Her Death

In the green master bedroom of a mock-Tudor house in the west end of the grey city of Toronto, a woman in late middle age lies dying, her pale arms almost as white as the sheet on which they are resting. It is April 24, 1942. Her failing body seems to her increasingly heavy, as if pulled by a great weight deeper and deeper into the flesh of the mattress. Outside, the air itself is weighted, saturated with the moisture of seasonal rain. Seeping into the room is the faintly discernible sound of the swollen river as it follows the path of the Humber Valley. The trees beyond the leaded windows have only just begun to show signs of spring.

In spite of what is about to happen, nothing in this room suggests struggle or discomfort: every cell of the woman's body seems not so much in rebellion against life as dissolving into death, the way the rain outside her door is willingly dissolving into the earth. Her body is at peace, has already accepted the verdict. But her mind is not as easy to subdue. Swinging back and forth between grief and rage, fear and crushing disappointment, it is like a compass needle trapped in a magnetic field. Often there is dread, always there is sorrow. Occasionally there is contempt: sometimes for herself, for what she sees as her whole deluded life; sometimes for others who have not met her expectations—her publishers, her business associates, the long line of people who have enjoyed the benefits of her career only to betray her in some way or for their own sorry purposes exploit the young female characters she has created. This misuse, she suspects, will not stop with her death; it will go on and on. It will be part of her legacy, her gift to the nation.

Beneath the carapace of the older adult she has become, the young girl she once was sometimes stirs, just as she has always done in happier moments, as if to suggest an alternative, more bearable narrative, a better life. But it is of no use. Here, in this suburban room on the cusp of a city, fiction cannot exist, and there is nothing to lighten the burden of memory. Only now and then does the recollection of an island home provide some consolation. This is a consolation of very brief duration, however, for she abandoned the sea-bound landscapes of her childhood, her young womanhood, long ago. She can barely recall now, here in this fashionable setting, the name or the face of the man who caused her to do so. But she knows he is pacing somewhere nearby and will be at her bedside when she least wants or expects him. There were children as well, children and the joy and disappointments they brought with them. They, too, are near, always changing, evolving into characters whose dialogue eludes her. She wanted to provide them with lovely sentences to say, wonderful things to do, but they have escaped her, entered the ordinary.

Suddenly she recalls a pastel dress she wore at fifteen, how it had changed her, lifted her from the ordinary. She had pasted a swatch of the material into her scrapbook, along with a lily of the valley from the path and a splinter from the steps leading to the clapboard hall where she had given the recitation. Dread moves through her veins as the page fades from memory. What has become of the book now? What has become of her desire to enshrine relics? What has become of the notion that everything in her life was charged with meaning, that the fragments she tore from experience to paste between the pages would in later life bring her joy? Even as she pasted, the pages were browning under the assault of time and oxygen. Now she has forgotten the lines she once knew by heart, the history of romance, the promise of the kind of everlasting beauty that overcomes the assault of time. She understands—has understood for years—the falseness of the formula. Everything crumbles and decays, and in the end becomes unmemorable.

But this not remembering makes her burn with shame. It is as if she were there again, a girl at the recital. She will not be able to deliver the poem, to perform. She will fail, humiliate herself in front of the neighbours and relatives gathered there to judge her. She will allow her father, watching eagerly from the audience, to see that she is not superior. She will be ordinary.

Was it Tennyson's "The Lady of Shalott"? she wonders. "'On either side the river lie . . .'" she whispers, but even whispering requires more breath than she can pull into this heavy, sinking body. "What have I done wrong," the young, slim reciting girl asks now, "that I should be required to carry this body with me for so long, like some kind of penance? You and your darknesses. You with your grim, adult scrapbooks filled with sinking ships and train wrecks, wars and family tragedies, mad husbands and unpredictable sons." A string of similar girls, all in pastel dresses, appears on the stage in the dying woman's mind; the Emilys and Annes and Rillas and Janes and Marigolds and Pats who have walked through the books. "What have we done wrong?" they ask, and then without waiting for an answer they chant, "'Long fields of barley and of rye.'" They sway, graceful as shafts of barley, shafts of rye, brushed by a soft, warm wind. "What have we done wrong?" they sigh. A Greek chorus of girls, filled with self-pity and accusation. I am not responsible for you and your troubles, the dying woman wants to tell them. And yet, and yet, she knows that they are she and she is them—or they are what she wanted to be, perhaps even once was. They are extraordinary. They are the antidote to the life she has lived, the life that paces nearby like a beast waiting to devour her, that will visit her when she least expects and least wants it. She can no longer bear her life. She can no longer bear the record of her life.

Suddenly she realizes that the poem she was required to recite was not "The Lady of Shalott" but "The Child Martyr," the story of a small Highland girl who dies protecting a hidden father. Where was he hiding? Somewhere in the darkest part of a rocky landscape, or perhaps in a sea of grass under a wide sky. She recalls the gestures that were part of the performance in the community hall and tries to raise her arm, as she had then, while whispering, "In *that* fair upper fold." She cannot move her arm. She could not, cannot, ever really find the hidden father.

Dean Priest, she thinks, Dean Priest was the difficulty. Dean Priest lied to her about her work, told her it was commonplace, when quite the opposite was true. She had burned the pages rather than submit to this ordinariness, rather than inhabit the common place, in the commonage.

Commonage. A word not unlike *parsonage.* And yet she lived long winters in a parsonage, in two separate parsonages, with madness pacing the floorboards above her. And why can she not remember the plot of the burned book? The book that Emily of New Moon burned. Her own name is Maud, she tells herself, not Emily. The Emily she invented on the page comes into focus, laughing. "I didn't marry him," the girl whispers. "I ran away. I fell in love."

All her young heroines had fallen in love, with the Gilberts and the Teddys or the ones who returned from the war. One of them fell in love in an orchard. They all had their dream houses and their charming children, their devoted house-keepers, their gardens, a brook running through the far end of the yard. But she had married Ewan. At last she is naming her own difficulty. "Ewan of Norval" doesn't work as a title. "Ewan of Leaskdale" doesn't work either. It doesn't work, didn't work. For a moment she thinks she can hear his voice delivering a disjointed, hysterical sermon in the next room. For a moment the grey, prosaic madness in the otherwise pretty houses of her married life in Leaskdale and Norval enters her mind. There had never been anything she could do to change the banality of that madness, those delusions, nothing except conjure some girls and their stories. *"The Story Girl,"* she remembers, naming aloud one of her most treasured creations. What was that girl's name? And who were all those children listening to her spin her yarns?

What was the difference between a yarn and a record? She had spun yarns and kept a record. Perhaps it was the word *kept*. The spun things were woven and then set free to float on the breeze, but the record, the truth, was kept. Volume after volume, year after year, she locked her journals away in cupboards and vaults, the truth of her days, the misery, recorded and kept, while the bright cloth of that which she had invented travelled the world on a warm, embracing breeze. Even the sorrow woven into the fiction was beautiful, touching, not the ugly grief of reality that no poetry can alter or elevate. What made her, of all people, want to keep those diaries, that enduring record of unhappiness?

She needed to write every day. Nothing had meant anything to her until it was written down. Yes, that was it: she had to write the day down, first, in the early days, to celebrate what had taken place, then later to keep the horror at bay—until the final few years, when nothing kept the horror at bay and at last the flow of words stopped, the ink dried, and silence and wordlessness entered her house. Like a woman in a poem, she had abandoned her work. "She left the web, she left the loom, / She made three paces through the room."

She attempts to move her limbs on the flat white slab of the bed. But her legs seem to have become too large, too heavy. It is as if, at its weakest, her body is enlarging rather than shrinking, all lightness smothered under a dark mass of expanding flesh and the reluctant circulation of blood. She recalls "The Lady of Shalott," how she had set her own unhappiness adrift, allowing it, allowing herself, to float downstream so that someone could admire its cold, pale face and long, perfect body. She recalls the child in the other poem, succumbing with joy to martyrdom. It will not be like that for her because there is nothing fluid here, nothing that yields to a current, and no transparency. "My mind is gone," she thinks, recalling some of the last words she had entered in her journals. "Such suffering and wretchedness." She is already sinking into the earth. She is longing, has always longed, for sleep.

Darkness is beginning to stain the room, but its progress is excruciatingly slow, like the first traces of autumn brown on a summer leaf. She would prefer the sudden, the catastrophic, a curtain flung angrily across the light, but knows this will not be permitted. She will be required to remember all she has forgotten before being granted her rendezvous with sleep; she will be required to commune with the ghosts of her previous selves: a small child in a dark dress being judged by her stern elders, a twenty-two-year-old teacher aching with desire in the arms of a young farmer, a long-suffering wife, a difficult mother but, most painfully, finally, an adolescent on a train moving toward, and later away from, a distant father.

Perhaps no father, no parent, could have satisfied her overwhelming desire for unconditional love, her monstrous, devouring perfectionism. Because, father or no father, she had always been, would always be, an orphan.

CHAPTER TWO

Orphan

Lucy Maud Montgomery did not, of course, remember her birth, but something in her believed that she did: the small frame house in Clifton, Prince Edward Island, welcoming her arrival; her father, Hugh John Montgomery, joyous; her mother, Clara Macneill Montgomery, young, weak but filled with delight. She did not remember her mother's death two years later, but she believed she remembered it as well. Her mother, she insisted, looked more beautiful in the coffin than the Lady of Shalott death-pale in her boat. Her mother's hands were long-fingered and white against a black silk dress. Her grief-stricken father had lifted little Maud up to the edge of the coffin so that the cherished face would remain imprinted in her memory forever. Pale blue eyelids, soft mouth, a brooch, the hairline above the high forehead. She wanted to believe she did not invent these fragments. "Maudie," she thought she heard her father say, "never forget this. Never forget."

Holding her, he promised to protect her, said that *he* would never forget, that he would stay forever. But he did not stay. He did not stay, and her first true memories were of her grandparents' farmhouse in Cavendish and the sternness with which she was raised. All her life in her fiction she would attempt to transform the acreage into a ravishing landscape lit by the kind of affection this man and woman were never able to give. Matthew and Marilla in the Anne books and Aunt Elizabeth and Aunt Laura in the Emily books were drawn as adults who were reluctant to express their love for the orphan, who hid it under a forbidding exterior, a revision or exaggeration on the author's part of the small amount of love she believed she received while growing up. In a way that seemed to elude Maud herself, her young protagonists almost always won over the harsh guardians who ruled them.

The men in Maud's stories were more benign, often taking straightaway to the girl-child in question and coming to act as her advocate, her defender. If they were fathers, they would, through no fault of their own, be separated from much-loved and adoring daughters. Most significantly, Emily, from *Emily of New Moon,* would begin a life devoted to literature by writing letters to her treasured and deeply mourned father. In *Jane of Lantern Hill*, Montgomery invented a father who, though absent, would be so complicated, promising, permissive, and attentive in his intermittent parenthood that she and every reader found it impossible not to love him. Sara Stanley, the gifted Montgomery-like narrator in *The Story Girl*, would, in the end, be happily reunited with her own beloved absent father.

Montgomery wanted this impossibility for herself all through her childhood, perhaps well into adulthood. Her thoughts and sometimes her diaries were filled with hopeful speculation concerning her own truant father. Seeing him again during a one-year stay in Prince Albert, Saskatchewan, in her early teens, after five years of separation, she writes, "Oh it is lovely to be with father again, though. He is *such* a darling. His eyes just *shine* with love when he looks at me. I never saw anyone look at me with such eyes before."

"But," she offers ominously, "I am afraid I am *not* going to like his wife."

Her visit was not wholly a success, in spite of some good times with young people her own age (as well as some uncomfortable times, when the pretty fifteen-year-old caught the unwanted attention of her high school teacher, Mr. Mustard). Over and over again, she ran into the displeasure of her stepmother, whom she first called "Mama," then "Stepmother," and finally "Mrs. Montgomery" as the relationship deteriorated between them. Names had potency in this domestic drama, and Maud was angry and hurt when her father was advised by his wife to stop calling his daughter "Maudie." The new Mrs. Montgomery thought it too childish. "I believe it is the affection implied in the diminutive of which she disapproves," young Maud wrote in her journal, adding, "I have already seen several displays of temper and sulkiness on her part towards father which were utterly unprovoked." Her desire to protect her father—or at least her version of him, his goodness, almost saintliness, in the face of an overbearing, bad-natured wife— was born at this time.

Yet she wrote very little about how this hen-pecked man interacted with her, his teenaged daughter, beyond his shining eyes and his beaming with pleasure when she showed him her first published poem. She may very well have had to invent many details of their relationship, though few of them made their way into the pages of her journal. It was as if, even then, she knew that wishful inventions should be put aside, kept somewhere else, for later use in fiction. Instead she wrote about her reactions to him, what he meant to her.

"I felt dreadfully over the thought of leaving father," she wrote as her year with him came to a close. "But then," she adds, "to go back to dear old Cavendish—I just *had* to feel glad about that."

She would love her distant, faintly remembered father all her life and would love, perhaps even more, everything she was able to invent about him because of his absence. He became a dominant feature in her imagination at a time when that imagination was rapidly developing. She could escape into him because he was not there. Her return to Cavendish and the home of her maternal grandparents allowed her, like "The Child Martyr," to preserve the image of the idealized father, keep him close by, carefully hidden in the cave of her vivid inner life whence he would emerge in fiction as one benign father figure after another. The humane and gentle Matthew in *Anne of Green Gables*, the eccentric yet compassionate Douglas Starr in *Emily of New Moon*, the grown-up Gilbert in the Anne sequels, and the permissive, intelligent, adoring, and mostly absent father in *Jane of Lantern Hill* would all have their source in Hugh John Montgomery. He died nine years after Maud's return to Cavendish. There is no evidence to suggest that throughout the intervening years she ever saw him again.

HER GRANDPARENTS Alexander and Lucy Macneill, on the other hand, were relentlessly present. Grim-countenanced, short on humour, drained by the effort of already having raised six children of their own, they must nevertheless have felt, beyond duty, a bewildered sort of affection for the strange, sensitive child who was thrust into the world of their declining years. And she, in turn, in spite of the claustrophobia engendered by it, was fully bound by the tribalism that was part of her inheritance on both sides of the family. Grandparents, aunts, uncles, and cousins would play significant roles well into her middle age. Even in her early teens, she would react with a kind of judgmental surprise when she discovered that someone's family was not as "clannish" as her own.

Loyalty to extended family would remain one of the prevailing themes in her life, overriding fame, society, intellectual companionship, and romance, and she would never question the right of even the most distant relative to turn to her in financial need. But as a child she could be crushed by the disapproval of the elder Montgomerys and Macneills. The Protestant world that formed her had been practically created in Prince Edward Island by these two families. They had both arrived in the eighteenth century and had not only helped transform the landscape from forests to fields, but also played a large part in the educational and political life of the developing community. Her great-grandfather William Simpson Macneill, rumoured to be the first male child born in Charlottetown, went on to serve as Speaker of the House in Prince Edward Island. Later, in 1874, the year she was born and just after Prince Edward Island became the seventh Canadian province to enter Confederation, her grandfather Donald Montgomery was appointed a senator by Sir John A. Macdonald. When the adolescent Maud was embarking on her journey to Prince Albert, Saskatchewan, it was Senator Montgomery who accompanied her on the trip out. Just before they left Charlottetown, he introduced her to "Premier Macdonald," who was touring the island at the time with his wife. "I can assure you I was quite excited over the prospect of seeing the Premier of Canada," Maud wrote in her journal, adding that he was "not handsome but pleasant faced." Her own grandfather, she confided proudly, was "a great crony of Sir John's."

In a world this small, the social and political pecking order was very visible, and even as a young child Lucy Maud Montgomery would have been extremely aware of her superior lineage, an awareness that would bring conflict and sorrow—as well as pride—all through her life.

Accompanying this awareness was the notion that it was status in a rural world, rather than an urban one, that really mattered. Most Canadians at the beginning of the twentieth century were still connected to the land and to the small towns and villages carved out of the bush only a century, at most, before. Status in such places was curiously unrelated to wealth, having more to do with ideas of loyalty, work ethic, thriftiness, an assumption of religious belief, and church attendance. Its hallmarks were discretion and pride. Even if there was money somewhere in the family, it was seldom discussed and never flaunted. The presence of large sums of money may even have been met with distrust, the suspicion being that sloth and wastefulness were part of the package. Whether one came from a "good" family was often determined not only by the behaviour of that family's members, but also by the state of their fields and the orderliness of their houses—both brought about by hard work rather than cold cash.

Maud placed great value on the manufactured landscape rather than the wilderness, on the fields and lanes and woodlots created by her pioneer ancestors. She gave such places romantic names, both in her fiction and in real life, like Lovers' Lane and the Lake of Shining Waters. She valued houses as well, referred to them by name, and gave them the same kind of careful attention she lavished on her young female protagonists. Places became almost characters in her books and in her life: in fiction, Green Gables, Silver Birch, New Moon, and Windy Poplars; in the actual world, Park

Corner, Sea View, and Journey's End. This personification of architecture led her to invest large amounts of emotion, and sometimes large amounts of money, in protecting places that she loved. But in the end, she could not stop each cherished place from disappearing from her life in the same way her parents had disappeared, either by perishing, as happened when the Macneill farmhouse in which she was raised was demolished, or by separation, as in the case of the Norval manse in southern Ontario, from which, after a score of years, she and her husband were banished.

Always these events were wrenching for Maud and reinforced her conviction that anything she loved was doomed. Underlying that conviction was something else, less openly admitted to, and that was her belief that nothing would, or perhaps could, fully rise to her standards. Perhaps it was not so much that the places and people she loved were doomed, but that they were doomed to let her down. One way or another they would abandon her. She could count on no one, on nothing. All her beloved places would change beyond recognition, and the relationships she most valued would end in disappointment or separation.

CHAPTER THREE

Love

All through her girlhood, young adulthood, and even into maturity, Lucy Maud Montgomery inspired romantic love in various people she knew. The first to fall under her spell was Nate Lockhart, a school chum, in 1889 when Maud was fifteen. It is easy enough to imagine how this pretty, intelligent, and highly imaginative girl might have captured the interest of a variety of boys, but Nate seems to have been the only young man courageous enough to tell her how he felt. She found him "a nice boy—clever and intellectual." But when he slipped her a note telling her that he loved her, she reacted with the same ambivalence and irritation the fictional Anne was later to feel when greeted with similar declarations from her schoolmate and rival Gilbert Blythe. The Nate and Maud story is similar in other ways to the fictional narrative of Anne and Gilbert. Nate, like Gilbert, was serious competition in the scholastic world. And although Maud eschewed his romantic advances, she nevertheless wanted—as did Anne with Gilbert—to keep his friendship. Nothing, however, came of this early skirmish, and Nate figured less and less in Maud's diary after she went to Saskatchewan in 1890 for the year with her father. Following her return to Prince Edward Island, Nate's name crops up now and then in her diary, but never in a romantic context.

The next to become enthralled was her high school teacher in Prince Albert, the much disparaged Mr. Mustard. "Well it's nearly 12 o'clock and I am just boiling over with rage," she wrote in the spring of 1891. "*Mr. Mustard was here again* tonight. That is the fatal secret! I can't, of course, pretend to be ignorant that it is I that he comes to see but surely he doesn't mean anything by it. I certainly hope not, anyhow." But mean something he did, and it wasn't long before Mr. Mustard "mustered," as Maud punned, the courage to ask whether she thought their friendship might develop into something else. Maud replied coolly, "I don't see what else it *can* develop into, Mr. Mustard."

This incident is intriguing for the contemporary reader. If today's Mr. Mustard was unwise enough to show such interest in a pupil, the consequences would likely be dire. No one in this scenario, however, if one overlooks the feelings of Mr. Mustard himself, seems to have been traumatized, least of all Maud. Soon she was back fraternizing with friends her own age at various socials and picnics while the prairie community around her buzzed with speculation as to whether Maud's teacher had been successful in his suit. In no time at all it would be apparent that he had not, and that Maud was much more interested in a young man called Willie Pritchard, the brother of her friend and confidante Laura.

"Tonight on the sofa I got Will to give me back my ring," she wrote playfully after an evening at the Pritchards', "but I promised to give it to him for 'keeps' tomorrow. He also asked me to give him a lock of my hair and although I pretended to refuse I *may* change my mind." It is clear from this and a number of other calculated moves that the teenaged Lucy Maud was very skilled at holding the attentions of a young man. Still, this suitor seems to have affected her on a level rather deeper than those who preceded him, and when it came time for her to leave Prince Albert she appears to have been genuinely saddened by the separation, and sad as well (if we overlook her dislike of her stepmother) to be leaving Saskatchewan. "I wonder if I shall ever come back to it. Perhaps I shall, if Will—but no, somehow, in spite of all, I can't think *that*—at least, not yet."

There is a poignant epilogue to this early romance. Six years later, when Maud was twenty-two and teaching in Belmont, Prince Edward Island, she received a letter from Laura Pritchard telling her that Will had died from "long and painful complications resulting from an attack of influenza some time ago." After receiving the news, Maud went to her trunk and dug out the "ten year letter" Will had written to her before she left Saskatchewan. (The idea behind such letters was that they were not to be opened until ten years had passed.) Will had suggested, when handing the epistle to Maud, that they might very well be able to read it together, but as Maud put it in her diary, in the intervening years they had "grown away from each other." So there, in Prince Edward Island, half a decade later, Maud read declarations of love from a boy who lay buried more than a thousand miles away.

By the time Will died, in 1897 in distant Saskatchewan, several gentlemen callers had come swarming around. Not the least among them was Maud's second cousin, an intelligent and nice-looking young man called Edwin Simpson, who in February of that year had declared his passion for her by letter. Maud replied that she did not feel the same way toward him, but she confessed in her diary that she believed the matter would come up again. Her suspicions were justified. On June 5, when Ed came home from college for a stay in Belmont, he proposed marriage.

He had many things to recommend him: he spoke and behaved well, he was presentable and educated, and he came from a good family, despite the fact that her clannish grandparents apparently despised all Simpsons. Most important, as Maud stated in her journal, "he was studying for one of the learned professions."

Maud accepted his proposal, though in her diary she confessed, "I knew I did not love him but I thought I *could*. I had never *really* loved anyone although I have had several violent fancies that did not last very long." She also knew that her grandfather in particular would heartily object, not only to the fact that Edwin was a relative (he had, according to Maud, "an almost morbid hatred of relations marrying"), but also because Ed was a Baptist, which according to Maud would be considered "as serious as if he had been a Mohammedan." Statements such as this reveal the very kind of aversion to change and suspicion of the "other" that would in time embed themselves in Montgomery's own personality, causing her conflict and shame and on occasion separating her from the richness of life.

Maud's own doubts about Ed Simpson began to grow. She had believed Ed was studying for law, or perhaps even a college professorship, and was more than a little put out when she learned he was intending to enter the ministry. Being a Baptist was bad enough, but being a Baptist minister was something altogether worse. "To marry a Baptist minister," she wrote, "would necessarily involve my re-baptism by immersion—a thing utterly repugnant to my feelings and traditions."

And there was something else, something more serious, though perhaps not considered vital at the time. "I remember the night of the 17th of June with a special distinctness," she wrote, "because it was the first night I became conscious of a feeling of *dislike* of Ed's caresses." It is difficult to know exactly how much physical arousal a young unmarried woman such as Maud, at the end of the Victorian era, could allow herself to acknowledge, but romance alone ought to have ruled out the "sense of physical repulsion" she claimed to have felt. "I looked," she admitted to her journal, "—and saw that I could not *bear* the mere touch of the man I had promised to marry!" Not long after this realization Maud broke off her engagement to Ed Simpson.

It might be possible to use this confession and her subsequent withdrawal from her fiancé, coupled with Maud's intense focus on female friendships—both in her life and her work—to support a theory that she may have been drawn to romantic and perhaps even physical connections with women rather than men. As a young girl, her attachments to her girlhood friends were often expressed in florid, romantic ways. Her terrible and relentless grief at the loss of her best friend and cousin Frede in 1919 might also be brought forward as evidence, were it not for the fact that the notion of "bosom friends," devoted to one another for life, was a staple of the Victorian era that had formed Maud and her associates. Moreover, this was a period when men were discouraged from being sensitive communicators, and Maud's passionate attachment to language, spoken as well as written, meant that she needed to *talk* in order to give and receive affection.

Sometimes, however, the need for a verbal expression of affection led her down strange paths, as evidenced by a bizarre and mystifying relationship that had developed in her middle years.

Shortly after moving with her husband, the emotionally fragile Ewan Macdonald, to Norval, Ontario, in 1926, Maud received a fan letter from a young woman called Isobel, a teacher who was living with her widowed mother and a sister less than a day's journey away. Maud knew that the letter, which was worshipful to say the least, was a little "too, too," but she also found it intelligent and in places "utterly delightful." And so she replied. Soon Isobel was sending "rather too expensive presents" and begging Montgomery to visit her and meet her family. Eventually Maud agreed, thereby getting herself in deeper and opening herself to a flood of passionate letters, parcels, phone calls, and invitations.

Finally a letter arrived in which Isobel confessed that her deepest desire was to sleep in the same bed with Maud. What is confusing about what follows is that, even after a fully judgmental Maud had reached the conclusion that Isobel was a "pervert" and "born under a curse as another girl might have been born cross-eyed or mentally deficient," she nevertheless visited Isobel and spent two nights in her bed, where she found "nothing to complain of." Maud subsequently decided that she had been "a nasty minded idiot to think of Isobel" as she had done.

Not surprisingly, a passionate letter arrived a week later in which lines such as "the sweet incense of your presence still broods around me like a dream" and "Darling, I love you so terribly, I do" figure prominently. Maud still did not end the relationship, and two years later she was complaining about advances from Isobel and claiming that she continued contact only because she was afraid of what might happen were she to stop. "I wish I dared give her a dose of rude truths," Maud wrote in her journal in 1932, "but I am really afraid of the consequences. I don't think it would take much to send her over the borderline into insanity—or suicide." Not much later, she did give Isobel what she saw as a dose of raw truths and accused her of being a lesbian. When Isobel replied with "reproaches and yowls of complaint," Maud attempted to end her correspondence with the girl, though she left the gate ajar by saying that if Isobel could content herself with "a sane friendship with an occasional friendly visit or letter," she would be "glad to respond." Soon Isobel was writing her "beloved darling" once again and Montgomery was complaining of feeling "hag-ridden" by her. The relationship, as far as we can tell, was ended once and for all with Montgomery's move to Toronto. In the last years of her life there is no mention of Isobel in any of the diary entries.

What was really going on in Montgomery's mind as she corresponded with and occasionally even visited this girl who was so obviously in the grips of an obsession? Maud was acutely aware of the dangers of continued contact, and yet something kept her from turning away. One can only speculate that given the state of her own home life, Ewan's fluctuating mental health, legal wrangles with neighbours and publishers, the deaths of several people she had been close to since childhood, and her ongoing problems with her children, this by now world-famous author craved affection to such an extent that despite her better judgment she was compelled to accept it even from such a precarious source. Maud wasn't likely to admit to this degree of neediness, either to Isobel or to herself in her diaries. (One must remember that Lucy Maud Montgomery knew very well that her diaries were likely to be published eventually, and that she edited and rewrote numerous entries with this in mind.) She may simply, in the final analysis, have succumbed to a curiosity about how this ridiculous situation would play itself out.

Whatever the case, it is certain that—despite her revulsion at Ed Simpson's caresses, her failure to mention in her diaries any sexual life with her husband, and later her ambivalent contact with Isobel—Montgomery was capable of intense heterosexual physical arousal. This certainty is due, in part, to what we know about the most passionate encounter of Maud's life.

During her tenure as a teacher in Belmont, Prince Edward Island, Maud boarded with the Leard family. She was acting as a substitute for six months in order to replace Al Leard, who had temporarily left his teaching post to receive further education, so the choice to reside with his family seemed a logical one. While there, Maud became friendly with the absent teacher's sister, Helen Leard, a young woman of about the same age—"We get along splendidly and have no end of fun," she wrote in her diary—and almost immediately she noticed something special about Helen's older brother, twenty-six-year-old Herman, who was "slight, rather dark, with magnetic blue eyes."

What followed, at the end of her engagement to Ed Simpson and just in advance of her grandfather's death, was riveting and painful, as these things are apt to be, but it also proved that Maud was a young woman capable of great longing and capable of appreciating the physical side of heterosexual love.

From the moment she met Herman Leard, Maud was studying his face, which, she wrote later in her diary, was "elusive, magnetic, haunting." At the same time, she was making judgments about his character, describing him brutally as having "no trace of intellect, culture or education— no interest in anything beyond his farm and the circle of young people who composed the society he frequented. In sober truth he was only a very nice, attractive, young animal! And yet!!"

And yet, indeed. After a few weeks of flirtatious teasing and joking, Maud took what she described as "the *first step* on a pathway of passion and pain" when during a drive home at night from a church meeting in Central Bedeque, Herman "leaned over, passed his arm about me and, with a subtly caressing movement, drew my head down on his shoulder." She wanted to "straighten up indignantly" but found herself utterly unable to do so, and the young man and woman remained in that position until the buggy reached the Leard farm, whereupon Maud jumped from the rig and ran up the stairs.

There followed a sleepless night filled with much confusion. Maud was "overwhelmed by a flood of wholly new and strange emotions" that she could "neither understand or control." The next night, coming back from a party in a neighbouring village, a similar event took place. Soon Herman was kissing her and sending "flame through every vein and fibre" of her "being." Where the kisses of Ed Simpson had repulsed her, Herman's awakened her sexuality and made her long for more.

None of this is particularly startling to those of us who came of age during the last decades of the twentieth century. After all, the two people involved were young and obviously attracted to each other, and their conduct was hardly scandalous. But to twenty-two-year-old Lucy Maud, these "wholly new and strange emotions" were anathema. Such was the complexity of Maud's personality that she could permit neither this romantic love, nor the physical attraction that accompanied it, to survive past its infancy. It was born, she recognized it as hers, and she named it accordingly. But she willed it out of existence before it could make any claims on her. The experience was wrenching and exhausting and gives us perhaps one of the clearest examples of how Maud was able, even under these overwhelming conditions, to pit herself against her real feelings and to conceal those feelings from those around her.

Alone in her room after a session of kissing, Maud vowed to stop the affair in its tracks. "It would be the rankest folly," she wrote in her diary some months later,

> to dream of marrying such a man. If I were mad enough to do so—well, I would be deliriously happy for a year or so—and wretched, discontented and unhappy all the rest of my life. I saw this plainly enough—passion, while it mastered my heart, left my brain unclouded. I never for a moment deceived myself into thinking or hoping that any good could come out of this love of mine.

Knowing what we do about her marriage to Ewan, we can only wish that passion had clouded her brain as well as her heart, and for a while it looked as if that might be the case. Several episodes full of an almost unbearable sexual tension followed, stolen moments by the fireside while the rest of the household slept, and then, not much later, stolen moments in her room. There was never any question about whether the relationship could become fully consummated—the times and Montgomery's strict upbringing would have made this impossible—and yet, as she wrote in her journal, she was aware that she was in danger of falling "over the brink of the precipice . . . into an abyss of ruin." She consequently "made a vow to break the chain that bound me at any cost—at any suffering."

For three weeks Maud kept out of Herman's way. Her soon-to-be ex-fiancé, Ed, had made a visit, and this, combined with her obvious ambivalence, caused Herman to avoid her as well. Montgomery guessed that the young man must have been confused and hurt by her behaviour—passionately responding to his caresses on the one hand and keeping herself aloof on the other—but she was determined to free herself from him. "I have an uncomfortable blend in my make up," she confessed in her journal, "—the passionate Montgomery blood and the puritan Macneill conscience."

Yet what really seemed to be reining in her relationship with Herman was a form of snobbery common to both the Montgomerys and the Macneills. In short, she believed that Herman Leard was not good enough for her. Still, when reading this section of the diaries, one wonders what made her believe that this was so. In spite of her allegations that Herman had little to recommend him in intellectual matters, he obviously came from a family whose reputation was good enough that neither the Montgomerys nor the

Macneills objected to Maud boarding in the Leard household. Eventually at least two of Herman's siblings would become educated and enter professional life, suggesting that Herman's family, and therefore Herman himself, was not entirely foreign to education. This young man was likely to become a successful farmer, not unlike Maud's own grandfathers. The two families that created Maud, excepting a senator and a Speaker of the House, had, after all, been wedded to the earth, and none of Maud's older relatives would have seen a rural life as something to be ashamed of. Moreover, it seems unfair on Maud's part to judge Herman's intellectual and verbal capacity when it was the "electric silences" between them that spoke most meaningfully to her, silences, as she wrote, "eloquent with a thousand tongues." Their attraction under the restraining circumstances in which they found themselves would have made conversation almost impossible. Had the relationship continued, Maud would likely have discovered at the very least a sensitive and perhaps cultured young farmer. And with time and exposure to Lucy Maud's literary interests, Herman might have wanted to become more acquainted with the world of books and the mind.

But Maud was determined to end it. After her grandfather's death, when she had returned to Cavendish and was no longer living in the Leard household, she would write: "He is dearer to me than ever," adding, "But I *will* conquer— I *will* live it down even if my heart is crushed in the struggle." And perhaps her heart really was crushed, for after this episode Maud became very pragmatic about love. Years later, at the end of January 1920, she would write in her journal about the various kinds of love, suggesting that there was a particular kind of love—a love not unlike the kind she had felt for Herman—which "in spite of its rapture and wonder and happiness" would somehow diminish the woman who lived under its influence. It would make her, she stated, "an absolute slave—and if the man so loved—the *Master*—were not something very little lower than the angels I think the result, in one way or another, would be disastrous for the woman." She made no secret of the fact, in several entries in the diaries, that she had never felt this kind of love for her own husband.

She never forgot Herman. "My own love for Herman Leard," she confessed in her diary two decades later, "though so incomplete, is a memory beside which all the rest of life seems grey and dowdy." Had she wanted to change her mind about Herman, however, she would not have been given the chance, for in 1899, one year after leaving Belmont and returning to Cavendish, Maud read in a local paper that

Herman Leard, like Will Pritchard before him, had died of complications from influenza. Maud responded with sorrow to this news, though not with anything resembling misgivings. Reading her diary entry, one cannot help but feel that the writer in Maud was watching herself react to the fatal news. Perhaps it is true that every artist, or certainly every literary artist, both experiences emotion and stands outside of that emotion in order to better understand it so that it can be transformed into art. The night after she heard of Herman's death, Maud appears a little too aware of the "dim, fragrant summer night, alight with calm stars" beyond the window where she knelt and thought of her abandoned lover lying in his coffin. She seemed, over and above grief, to be intent on creating an almost stereotypical picture of the tragic heroine. Ever since childhood, romantic lines written by a senti-mental Victorian poet called Mrs. Hemans had had a great effect on Maud:

> The sounds of the sea and the sounds of the night
> Were around Clotilde as she knelt to pray
> In a chapel where the mighty lay
> On the old Provencal shore.

There is more than a little of Clotilde in the image Maud now created on the page, though whether she created it for herself or for her future readers, or both, is something we will never know.

And in 1929, on a trip to Prince Edward Island, passing the church graveyard where he was buried, she "had the oddest feeling that Herman Leard was *reaching out to me from the grave*—catching hold of me—drawing me to him." This strong feeling visited her in spite of the fact that, as she wrote, she was past menopause and therefore, from her point of view, past the age when such physical attachments should mean anything to her. And then again, in 1931, when copying the diary entries concerning Herman, she found herself once more in thrall. "I had gone back over thirty years," she wrote. "And I wanted to *stay* back there—with Herman and youth and *life*." Yet even at that late date she reiterated her claim that Herman had not been up to her standards. "I think I did well to resist it," she wrote, "and escape it as far as I did—thanks to the powerful passions of pride and ambition that were my birthright."

It is both fascinating and disturbing to conjecture that Montgomery, in rejecting Leard, was really rejecting the rural island life for which she felt such affection and which she would mine over and over again in her fiction. Her life would always be one of contradictions, of self-imposed exile, and of fantasy. It is possible that the beloved landscape she had abandoned had to be kept, like a muse, at a distance in order to see it whole and to mythologize it, or at the very least idealize it. Or perhaps this rejection was born of the colony dweller's belief that places and people beyond the borders of one's birthplace are more important and therefore more meaningful. In Montgomery's case, by never fully accepting Herman Leard while at the same time admitting her passion for him, she may have been both dismissing and embracing home. She utterly refused to live the rural life offered to her by the island on which she was born, and yet she would return to that island repeatedly in her imagination as a setting for her art.

Another intriguing and mystifying detail concerning the episode with Herman Leard has been brought to light recently by Mary Rubio in her meticulously researched biography *Lucy Maud Montgomery: The Gift of Wings*. According to local people Rubio interviewed some years ago, Herman Leard, like Maud herself, was engaged to someone else during the time their relationship blossomed. Not a word about this is in Maud's journals. Maybe pride prevented her from commenting on the situation, or perhaps the fact of Leard's engagement did not sit well with the romantic picture that Maud—likely after the fact—was attempting to draw. Questions arise, then, as they always seem to with Montgomery, about the fiction she injected into her journals, and conversely, the elements of actual life that, consciously or unconsciously, she permitted to pass through the portal of her imagining into the realm of invented narrative.

CHAPTER FOUR

In a Man's World

As a young woman, having excelled at the exams that would allow her entrance into Prince of Wales College in Charlottetown, Lucy Maud Montgomery became, upon graduation, a teacher for one year. She then attended Dalhousie University for a term before accepting a post in 1897 as a teacher in Belmont, Prince Edward Island. When her grandfather died suddenly in 1898, however, she would feel duty bound to return to Cavendish to live with her grandmother, and would leave the older woman's side only once, to work at the *Halifax Daily Echo*. After half a year at the newspaper, Montgomery would once again be called to Prince Edward Island by her grandmother's need, and she would live with the strong-willed and now thoroughly dependent old lady until her grandmother's death eight years later, in 1911. As limiting as it may have been for a young woman with many social and intellectual interests, the situation nevertheless provided Montgomery with the quiet and order she required to pursue her literary work seriously.

Emily Byrd Starr, the protagonist of Montgomery's trilogy *Emily of New Moon*, *Emily Climbs*, and *Emily's Quest*, and the character who most resembles Montgomery herself, saw her own ambition to become a published writer as a kind of fevered calling, a spiritual vocation of sorts, not unlike the life embraced by certain female saints. The way to success in this vocation is compared by her—as it is by Montgomery in her autobiographical book *The Alpine Path*—to climbing upward toward a magical summit. At the beginning of the ascent, the acceptance of a poem in a seed catalogue is cause for much rejoicing. And when Emily's cousin Jimmy sends her first novel off to an American publisher in a biscuit box and the publisher accepts the previously much rejected manuscript, there can be, for Emily, no greater joy. She becomes, quite literally, like any good saint, ecstatic.

Emily's creator must have reacted similarly when in April 1907 the L.C. Page Company of Boston accepted her first novel, *Anne of Green Gables*, for publication. Montgomery's manuscript had already been rejected by a number of publishers, then shut away in a closet for at least a year, then mailed out again and again. It was easy enough to do this in privacy. The local post office was operated out of her grandmother's kitchen, so both the many hopeful mailings and the equally plentiful and humiliating returns could be hidden. Finally, one of the slim envelopes that made the fictional Emily's heart so glad (they were not fat enough to contain a spurned manuscript) arrived in the morning delivery. In that envelope was an offer from Page to "add the book to our next season's list."

This crucial event took place at a moment in Montgomery's life when almost everything around her was in flux. Her grandmother, the only consistent parental figure in her childhood, was old and ill, and Maud was required to act as full-time caregiver, and presumably postal clerk as well. The home that she and her grandmother cherished was literally collapsing, its roof leaking in dozens of places and plaster falling from the ceilings. Montgomery must have known that both grandmother and house would be in her life only a little longer, since she was certainly aware that by the terms of her grandfather's will, her uncle John Macneill was to inherit the house as well as the farm. John's strong personality left Montgomery in little doubt that he would be both swift and brutal about claiming the property once his mother died. Most significantly, however, she had become semi-secretly engaged to the Presbyterian minister, Ewan Macdonald, on the understanding that she would not be able to marry until her grandmother's death. Into this turbulent weather pattern plunged the lightning bolt of an answered prayer: she was soon to be the author of a published book.

How harsh and stark that whole winter must have been: the crumbling, ill-maintained house; the bad-natured, greedy uncle; the slowly dying old woman who, despite her illness, would not allow more than one room to be heated at a time; the snow drifting in the farmyard; the orphan-spinster imprisoned by duty; the frosted panes of the windows keeping out much of the light. Her situation might have inspired a novel like *Ethan Frome*, and yet the woman who endured that claustrophobic season, and a decade of seasons like it, had just received an offer to publish *Anne of Green Gables*, while Edith Wharton, who at that very moment may well have been finishing up *Ethan Frome* (published 1911), was surrounded by servants and formal gardens at her exquisite Massachusetts estate. And while Wharton would be able to look deeply into the dark heart of North American rural severity as well as into urban privilege in her writing, Lucy Maud Montgomery would never, in her novels, be able to confront head-on the sometimes grim realities of her own existence.

One can only imagine Maud's joy, however, when that letter entered her bleak kitchen. And the reason one can *only imagine* it is because, uncharacteristically, she did not write much about it in her diary. Two radically life-changing events had taken place: her engagement to Ewan and the acceptance of her manuscript. Although she did report her literary success to her western pen pal Ephraim Weber, a writer with whom she established a lively, lifelong correspondence, the diary makes no mention of the forthcoming publication until three months after Page's initial letter. It was not until August 1907 that she confessed what she had been up to. "On April 15th," she declared, "I received a letter from the L.C. Page Co. of Boston accepting the MS of a book I had sent them and offering to publish it on a royalty basis!" As for her engagement to Ewan, it is referred to only briefly and, it would seem, in passing.

There are any number of reasons why this might be so. Superstitious by nature, Maud may have decided not to dwell on either occurrence until she was fully married on the one hand and fully published on the other. These happy events may also have made her even more secretive than usual, and she may have been loath to record them in her journal on the slim chance that someone might read the pages in question. (In the first entry of these journals, written when Maud was fourteen, she announces, "*And*—last but *not* least—I am going to keep this book locked up!") Or, what seems more likely, judging by what we know of Montgomery's editing and rewriting of the diaries—sometimes years or decades after the events being written about took place—and in view of what happened later, especially in relation to L.C. Page, Montgomery may very well have decided to remove any references to her effusive reaction. Her experience with Page was very unpleasant indeed, and over the years there is plenty in the diary about the unfolding of this long and miserable affair.

In essence, Maud, likely in a rush of excited enthusiasm, quickly signed a contract giving over all rights, including film, dramatization, serialization, and translation rights, to L.C. Page in return for a royalty of 10 percent on the wholesale price once more than 1,000 copies had been sold. Page also strongly suggested—almost insisted—she begin work on a sequel, while at the same time holding the author to a five-year first-refusal clause. This arrangement served to bind her to creating Anne sequels for years to come.

The success of *Anne of Green Gables* when it was published in May 1908, and, it would seem, from that day forth, hardly needs mention. And in accordance with Page's wishes, *Anne of Avonlea* was released to an eager audience by the fall of 1909. Among her fans Lucy Maud Montgomery could now count poet Bliss Carman, Governor General Earl Grey, and Mark Twain, who announced that "In 'Anne of Green Gables' you will find the dearest and most moving and delightful child since the immortal Alice." The reviews on both sides of the border were gratifying to say the least, but it was the positive reaction of male authority figures that Montgomery would need to hold on to and remember in the face of what occurred later in her career.

Her royalties made her financially—though not emotionally—independent. She waited, mostly in vain, for some kind of approbation from her family and her community regarding her achievement. While some of the more educated members of the clan demonstrated a new-found respect for Maud and her "scribbling," others were ominously silent. Mystifyingly, the records of the local literary club that she helped to found make no reference to her success, a slight that must have been deeply hurtful. In truth, her accomplishments made little or no difference to the responsibilities and duties of her daily life. Still tied to her grandmother and the old house, she attempted to repair disintegrating plaster with cheese-cloth, and she was semi-traumatized when a spark from the kitchen stove set the troublesome roof on fire and she was obliged, single-handedly, to quench the flames. The image of a lone woman encumbered by heavy Edwardian skirts climbing a ladder with full buckets of water in her hands is almost impossible to conjure up, but somehow Maud was able to avert disaster.

What she seemed completely unable to do at his time, even after the extraordinary success of *Anne of Green Gables*, was to act as her own advocate, either personally or professionally. This may have had something to do with the sense of powerlessness felt by many women at the time. Women were not able to vote in Ontario until 1917, and although Maud marked her first visit to the polls in her diary: "On Monday December 17th, I polled my first vote!" she could not bring herself to believe that a significant change of status would result. "I suspect," she wrote, "that matters will jog on in pretty much the same way for a good while yet," after confessing that she had never "felt any particular interest in politics." Or perhaps, like many Presbyterians, she believed she did not deserve her good fortune, that in some essential way she had not really earned it. She had, after all, thoroughly enjoyed writing *Anne of Green Gables*, and in her world pure enjoyment was not expected to result in much that was good.

Less enjoyable was the series of sequels Page subtly bullied her into writing, sequels that arrived like babies every one or two years: *Anne of Avonlea, Anne of the Island, Anne's House of Dreams*. Writing the character that had originally so delighted her became a chore. And yet when Page asked for more, Lucy Maud, accustomed to duty, obligingly returned to her writing desk and her red-haired heroine.

Late in 1910 she visited her publisher-taskmaster at his stately home in Boston, oddly echoing Charlotte Brontë's famous trip from Haworth to London. (It is quite possible that Montgomery herself might have made the connection, as in 1911 she noted in her diary that she had been rereading Elizabeth Gaskell's biography of the famous Yorkshire author.) While there, Montgomery was introduced to writers, entertained at dinners and receptions, taken to concerts, and encouraged to visit the halls of fashion. Louis Page was a charming host, and his attentions to Maud paid off, at least for him. Before she left Boston for Prince Edward Island, he persuaded her to sign another contract extending her obligation to his company by a further five years.

The result was decades of betrayal on Page's part and nerve-racking lawsuits on Montgomery's. In 1918 she sued Page for unpaid royalties, eventually settling for $18,000, in return for which she signed over all rights to *Anne of Green Gables* in perpetuity. Shortly thereafter, opportunistic as always, Page sold the film rights for $40,000 and then promptly, and without the author's permission, published *Further Chronicles of Avonlea*, using stories that had been cut from the original *Chronicles of Avonlea* and making sure to place the image of a red-headed girl on the book's cover. Legal action concerning this last move on the American publisher's part would continue for years, with countersuits and appeals following on the heels of lawsuits until, in 1925, the New York State court decided in Montgomery's favour. In 1927 the case was audited, and the results determined that Page owed Montgomery $16,000. Finally, in 1928, Montgomery's lawyer wrote to say he had taken the steps necessary to force Page to pay the sum.

In the beginning, Page undoubtedly believed that because Montgomery was a woman, and one from an unsophisticated corner of the world, she would give him little trouble over terms that clearly favoured his company, and initially Maud's eagerness to be published must have given him every reason to believe this. It is unlikely he would have taken such risky liberties had she been a man educated at Harvard or Princeton and living in Philadelphia or New York. He must have been unpleasantly surprised, then, by her developing nerve and, as time went by, tenacity. Five lawsuits and countersuits unfolded over a period of ten years, flooding in and out of Maud's life like a series of toxic waves. Often she would leave a letter from her solicitor unopened for several days, knowing the sleeplessness and anxiety that would result if the contents were unsettling. But she did not give in. Here, after all, was something she might be able to control. Set next to the uncertainties of a motherless childhood, an emotionally complicated husband, and unpredictable sons, legal battles may have seemed like a contest she had at least a chance of winning and may also have provided a much-needed outlet for residual anger. Victory, when it finally arrived in the form of the $16,000 settlement, would have been enormously satisfying and must also have settled a few psychological scores, both past and present.

Her next battle would be neither satisfying nor successful and would nudge Montgomery's literary reputation into a downward spiral from which it would not recover until years after her death, if indeed it ever recovered. It was a battle that many women writers had already been forced to fight— with varying degrees of success—and one that still, now and then, shows signs of recurring whenever a posse of self-appointed learned literary men decide that a certain style should dominate and then try to insinuate that style, and those who practise it, into a dominant position in the canon. The 1920s and 1930s saw the pantheistic romanticism of Wordsworth and Coleridge start to fade as modernism came into fashion in the English-speaking world. A group of men in Canada, true to their colonial nature, picked up the trend from Mother England and Father America and began to demand change. Montgomery, a woman writing, they believed, for an audience of adolescent girls, was one of the first to be dismissed. They abhorred the very idea of her works, or at least they thought they did. There is little evidence of careful critical dissection of either her subjects or her style.

This ambivalence toward women's writing, and even toward the very existence of female authors, was certainly not new. One thinks of Thomas Wentworth Higginson advising Emily Dickinson not to publish at all, or to publish only when Higginson himself had manipulated her verse into a form acceptable to the conventions of the day. Charlotte Brontë had received even more radical advice from the Romantic poet Robert Southey, who, replying to a letter she wrote to him from Haworth Parsonage, suggested that she give up writing altogether and confine herself to more womanly pursuits. One also remembers the group of male writers in the Canadian West in the 1970s declaring that Carol Shields's work was too housebound and domestic for their taste and not, therefore, to be taken seriously. (These allegations were made *before* Shields won the Pulitzer Prize, which established her international literary reputation.) Words such as *contemporary, urban*, and *realism* are often tossed about at such moments. Sometimes words such as *cosmopolitan* and *universal* are used against a woman as examples of everything that the male "experts" decide her work is not, and words such as *sentimental* and *romantic* and *lush* are used to describe the various sins she and her writing have committed.

Montgomery was a sitting duck for all of this. Given to writing about landscape and how it shapes character, she was accused of writing purple prose. Because many of her books focused on the coming of age of adolescent girls, her work was exempted from serious literary discourse and she was compared to the authors of such one-dimensional books as *Pollyanna* and *Rebecca of Sunnybrook Farm*. She was particularly attractive as a target because almost everyone in Canada knew her name—even those who had not read her books—and many, many people, of all ages and both genders, *had* read and delighted in her fiction. A "popularity" survey conducted by Montreal's *Family Herald and Weekly Star* in 1937 placed Charles Dickens and Lucy Maud Montgomery at the top of the list of most widely read authors, guaranteeing that envy would erupt among some of her peers. Even though later in her life, after her move to Toronto, she became active in developing the Canadian Authors Association, most of her creative work was completed either in a farmhouse in Prince Edward Island or in a manse in rural Ontario, ensuring that she would not be part of a literary movement on the one hand, or a literary coterie on the other, and would not, therefore, be afforded the relative safety that numbers might provide. She was not aligned with any academic institution and thus could not carry much authority in what would turn out to be a quasi-academic set of arguments. Once the words *cosmopolitan* and *universal* were used, there was no one to point out the obvious irony that Montgomery was one of a very few Canadians at the time who was published and admired in literally dozens of foreign countries. In short, she was on her own and had to stand by helplessly as her writing came under fire.

Most damning of all was the notion that she wrote only for an audience of young girls. This was, and is, of course, not true. Without serious mental effort I can think of at least three male writers who have told me how much Montgomery's work has meant to them. One of these men, writer and scholar Stan Dragland, recently said that he had become interested in Montgomery as a result of a teacher reading aloud in class. "She read a girl's book and a boy's book," he told me. "The girl's book was *Anne of Green Gables* and the boy's book was . . ." His inability to recall either the title or the author says a great deal about how foolish gender specificity in relation to literature really is. Quality is, or should be, the only determinant. Poet Bliss Carman, Prime Minister Stanley Baldwin, author Mark

Twain, and Governor General Earl Grey had all publicly endorsed Montgomery's work, but this was quickly forgotten by the men bent on attacking her.

The man leading the charge was William Arthur Deacon, a fierce proponent of modernism and, at the time, a force to be reckoned with. Although educated as a lawyer, Deacon moved with enthusiasm into the world of Canadian literary criticism as a book review editor for a number of influential publications, including the *Manitoba Free Press* and *Saturday Night* magazine, cementing his career, and his power, as books editor for *The Globe and Mail* (and for its predecessor, the *Mail and Empire*) from 1928 to 1961.

Ruthless in his scorn toward Montgomery and her writing, he forced her not only out of serious literary consideration, but also out of the Canadian Authors Association for which she had worked so hard, and in which, one imagines, she was hoping to find a like-minded community. As vice-president of the Toronto chapter in 1937, Maud must have felt at least partly included and respected. However, when Howard Angus Kennedy, the president of the organization, died in 1938, Deacon took the opportunity to shake up the executive of which he was a vocal part. After an association meeting in April 1938, Montgomery returned home to write in her journal that she had been "elbowed out" in a manoeuvre Deacon had "planned very astutely." She observed that "Deacon had always pursued me with malice" and that she was happy to "no longer work with him."

Among the literary men marching by Deacon's side were Professor Pelham Edgar, chair of the English and French departments at the University of Toronto and an advocate of modernism, and Ontario critic Arthur Phelps, who asserted that Montgomery's work was naïve and provincial and who wrote that her readers were "uncultured and unsophisticated." What this boys' club failed to predict and ultimately did not live to see was that Montgomery's writing was to be seminal in the development of later Canadian literature, especially that written by women. Through the two themes she dealt with most—the domestic world established by our pioneer forebears and the burgeoning creative life in that world, usually represented by a gifted young woman trying to make a mark—her work put forward the notion that these two ideas need not be mutually exclusive. Upper-middle-class colonial professionals with centrally heated brick houses and dependable salaries would have had no experience of the lives Montgomery chose to depict, nor would they have wanted any. Most likely they would have felt superior to the people with whom Montgomery lived for the greater part of her life and whose eccentricities and frailties she so sensitively and wittily explored, especially in her minor characters. In short, misogyny would not have been the only factor at work here. Class snobbery would have been part of the package as well.

But what Montgomery achieved in books such as *Emily of New Moon*, where a young woman with a startlingly original voice and vision actually succeeds as a writer, or *Rilla of Ingleside*, the only Canadian novel that centred around life on the home front during the First World War, was more groundbreaking than any idea of modernism borrowed from larger and allegedly more important countries. Essentially, she gave permission to succeeding generations of Canadian writers to mythologize their dusty small towns and marginal farms, their daily lives and those of their seemingly unexceptional neighbours. In this way, it is not an exaggeration to suggest that without the books of Lucy Maud Montgomery, which she had read as an adolescent, Alice Munro's own books might not exist, or might exist in a very different form. A truly great artist should be remembered for her influence on that which follows as much as she is remembered for her work.

Montgomery's influence was considerable, and not only in Canada. All over the world readers responded, and continue to respond, not only to the "spirit," but also to the "spiritedness" of her writing. Perhaps most important is the universal perception provided by Montgomery's work that the imagination is a liberating force in the face of oppression, whether that oppression is exemplified by a collection of unyielding and controlling adults or a rigid totalitarian regime. No one is truly powerless as long as they possess an inner life. Montgomery and her many readers knew this, even if her critics did not.

The celebrated Canadian writer Robertson Davies bore unbiased witness to Montgomery's universality. In *The Peterborough Examiner* at the time of her death, he wrote, "Nations grow in the eyes of the world less by the work of their statesmen than their artists. Thousands of people all over the world are hazy about the exact nature of Canada's government . . . but they have clear recollections of *Anne of Green Gables.*" There is, we should add, next to no one anywhere beyond the halls of academe who has any "clear recollection" of either Deacon or Edgar.

Apart from one or two outbursts during which she makes reference to a man "who is no friend" of hers, Montgomery does not go deeply in her diaries into her fall from critical grace, indicating once again how aware she was of future readers and how much she hoped that time would undo what Deacon and his friends set out to achieve. But this group of men had been very successful in their endeavours, and it would take years to undo the damage to her reputation.

Not until the late 1960s, more than twenty years after Montgomery's death, would Professor Elizabeth Waterston write the first scholarly article that dealt with Montgomery's work as serious literature. And according to Waterston's colleague Mary Rubio, even then, shortly after completing her article, Waterston was approached by a well-meaning and distinguished male colleague who encouraged her to abandon altogether the subject of Montgomery and her work. If one wanted to climb the ladder of academic success, he insinuated, it would be best to place that ladder against a more substantial wall.

Happily, instead of heeding the warnings, Elizabeth Waterston and Mary Rubio spent the next several decades studying Montgomery. Not only did they publish papers and arrange conferences, they undertook the enormous task of editing and publishing five volumes of Montgomery's journals. Later they published important books on Montgomery—most recently Rubio's biography and Waterston's *Magic Island: The Fictions of L.M. Montgomery*. Under their supervision, a vast Montgomery archive was assembled at the University of Guelph, one that is now, seventy years after the author's death, much visited.

Thanks to scholars such as Rubio and Waterston in Guelph, and the dedication of Dr. Elizabeth Epperly in Prince Edward Island, more and more academic investigation is taking place around Montgomery's work. Almost completely forgotten now, Edgar and Deacon are no doubt turning in their graves because of this, but what would cause them even greater unrest is the recently reported fact that since its publication in 1908 *Anne of Green Gables* alone has to date sold more than 50 million copies worldwide.

CHAPTER FIVE

Sorrow

As a very young woman, Lucy Maud Montgomery recorded the details of her daily life in a number of ways: in scrapbooks and diaries and, perhaps most intriguingly given that she began this activity at a time when few young women took photographs, through the lens of a camera. All three means of record-keeping would become habits for life. The scrapbooks and the diaries became darker as she grew older, but surprisingly, in spite of the troubles that plagued her, there was almost always something hopeful and optimistic about the pictures. In a sense, the visual record corroborates more than almost anything else the sincerity of her fictional writings, indicating that the love of the perceived world in general, and of landscape in particular, that manifests itself over and over again in her female characters, and sometimes in her male ones, was a real and significant aspect of her own personality.

She photographed the corners of her childhood room, the kitchen of the Macneill farm, the garden in front of the old house, a number of cats, various lanes leading to and from the property, the view out her window, the items on her dressing table, friends on the seashore, supper tables surrounded by cousins, herself in her trousseau, a corner of the parlour, woodland scenes, meadows and pastures, her much-loved cousin Frede. Fences, gates, and bridges. China dogs, heirloom jugs, empty rocking chairs, brand-new cars, wood-burning stoves, schoolhouses, and meeting halls. While she lived with her grandmother in Cavendish, Maud developed her photographs herself in a makeshift darkroom.

Later, after she had moved with her husband to Ontario, and once her boys were born, there would be the usual array of baby pictures, as well as photos of the manses at Leaskdale and at Norval and, later, the house in Toronto she would call Journey's End. At the same time as she was photographing these houses and their gardens, she would venture beyond to document the features of the surrounding landscape: a grouping of fir trees on a nearby hill, a river valley, narrow country roads lined by maple trees, churches, meeting halls, or the crossroads at the centre of a village. There is something about photographs taken by amateurs that causes us to believe that the person behind the camera loved or at least admired the subject on which the lens was trained. With Maud, however, although affection would have played a significant part, we cannot help feeling that her desire for changelessness and her need for control also contributed to the impulse to click the shutter.

Set against the diary entries from the same periods of her life, the photographs can be jarring or at the very least confusing. Ewan, for example, during some of the most difficult periods of their marriage, looks ever the sweet-tempered, well-dressed, and slightly shy country clergyman. At a time when his mother was driven to distraction by his philandering, her son Chester appears dashing and courteous, a true gentleman. And once, right below a lengthy description in her journal of searing despair and helpless panic attacks, with what seems to be a considerable amount of pride and a remarkable lack of irony, she pasted three photos of the progression of ivy growing on the wall of her house. This kind of bifurcating reaction on Montgomery's part to almost everything she encounters comes up again and again and is one of the most exasperating and fascinating features of her character. Were it not for the extreme nature of each of these conflicting reactions, her stance might almost be called ambivalent. But because the term *ambivalence* suggests at least some measure of uncertainty, it is a word that is almost impossible to associate with the adult Lucy Maud Montgomery. Passionate about her point of view, regardless of the contradictions contained within it, Maud would plunge down first one path then another, seemingly unaware of obstacles ahead, or perhaps wanting future readers of her journals to believe she was unaware and therefore innocent. There are several moments in the diaries when one does not entirely trust her reliability, especially during the passages written long after the fact.

This is not so with the photographs. Right or wrong, we feel manipulated neither by the images nor by the suggestion of the pleasure Montgomery must have felt while taking them, as we sometimes do when reading the journals. Her eye—her "vision"—is more closely tied than is her considerable intellect to the creative impulse that went into making her art. This may account for the fact that many of Montgomery's readers retain vivid memories of rooms and views, streams and fields, and an assortment of woodlands and orchards long after the peculiarities of personality attached to the characters that inhabit the books have begun to fade.

But there is one photograph, taken in winter far from home, that disturbs rather than delights. It is a stark, full-frontal view of the cold wrought-iron gates at the entrance to the driveway of Macdonald College in Montreal, where her cousin Frede was employed, a photograph that tells us more about Montgomery's terror and sorrow than all the words written in the diary at the time. These are no ordinary gates. Slightly ajar, they are forbidding and brutally strong. Closed, they would be utterly impenetrable. Placed as they are at this point in the journals, the reader knows that to Montgomery they would have served as a metaphor for almost everything in her life that was impossible to bear.

ONCE, IN A FIT OF PIQUE, the misguided, obsessed, and much-maligned Isobel had written that Maud did not know how to love. She doubted, she said in a letter, that Maud loved "anybody except your boys, your cat, and, I presume, your husband." This, like almost everything Isobel said or did in relation to Montgomery, was extreme. And yet there was something in it. Although Montgomery repeatedly claimed that she had never loved Ewan in a romantic way, she must have been genuinely fond of him. She truly loved her children—often in a controlling and manipulative way, it is true—but in a constant and motherly way as well. And she was nothing if not passionate about cats.

Her earliest scrapbook is, among other things, a testament to her fondness for felines. In it she pasted decals, chromolithographs, and magazine illustrations of cats and kittens at their most beguiling: tangled up in balls of wool, wearing ribbons round their furry necks, gazing regally into space, or snuggling in the warm arms of a delighted child. As a child she cut a sample of fur from each of the many cats who lived in and around the farmhouse in Prince Edward Island and, after tying the small tufts with tiny pieces of silk thread, pasted the fur onto the page along with a record of the cat from whose coat it had come.

It is not difficult to conjecture that young Maud might have found the unconditional love she so badly needed in the affection of these animals; that, plus a physical warmth not likely present in her relationship with her grandparents. Whatever it was about cats, Maud never outgrew her fondness for them. Over the years, she would consistently be drawn to them and want to make them a significant part of her domestic life.

The first cat to appear with any frequency in her diaries was Daffy, who had been with Maud in Prince Edward Island and was shipped to the Leaskdale manse shortly after Maud and Ewan set up housekeeping there. He lived on in the company of the family and was greatly mourned by all when, at fourteen years of age, he met an unhappy end after a hunter mistook him for a groundhog. But one cat in particular, Luck, was an object of intense devotion in Maud's middle years. A source of comfort and affection in the Macdonald home, Luck slept on Maud's bed every night, greeted her effusively when she returned from trips both long and short, was extensively photographed (either alone or in the company of everyone Maud felt was important in her life), and provided some laughter when things were not going well, which by the time Luck was in his middle years was often. She loved, as she stated in her journal, to hear him purring on her lap or to reach out "and feel his silken flank in the darkness." And he was singular. "After Luck came to me," she wrote in her diary, "I never cared for any other cat. Cats before him I have loved as *cats*. Luck I loved as a human being."

The biography of Luck, which Maud wrote in her diary a year after his death during the miserable winter of 1937, is touchingly human and heartfelt. Over fifteen pages long, it details every aspect of Luck's life: his physical beauty, dignified temperament, hunting prowess, unshakable loyalty, perfect manners, favourite retreats, love of windows and boxes, reasoning powers, and various engaging eccentricities. And over and over again in this chronicle, Maud speaks of her sense of loss. "I have wanted to write everything I could down about Lucky," she stated, "—not to forget one of his charms and dear ways and lovelinesses. Everyone will soon forget him but me. I shall never forget him."

And she never did. More than twenty photographs of Luck are pasted in the diary, both throughout the account of his life and death as well as here and there on other pages, along with a photo of his birthplace in Prince Edward Island. Years later she would bemoan his loss, claiming that her trials would have been softened by his presence. And she never got over his absence. Although he had lived for fourteen years, Maud found she could not be philosophical about his death and did not seem to register, even in the face of increasingly painful personal problems, the irony of his name. "No matter how old he was," she wrote, "he would still be *Luck*. Just to have had him for another year even." At one point she added bitterly, "I hope, in my next incarnation, I shall not be the passionate lover I have been in this. I hope I shall not love pets or people or places as I do."

Near the beginning of the entry about Luck, Maud announced significantly, "Nothing since Frede's death has caused me such grief and anguish." In spite of what the rejected Isobel might have wanted to believe, Lucy Maud Montgomery had been quite capable of forming loving and meaningful friendships. One woman in particular, her cousin Frederica (or Frede, as she was called), was vitally important to her, as a companion, a confidante, and as someone with whom she could laugh and have fun. This was not the variety of attachment that Isobel either consciously or unconsciously hoped for, but as an intimate friendship, it was for Montgomery, and one imagines for Frede, pure delight. All her notions about "kindred spirits and bosom friends" that were to appear particularly in *Anne of Green Gables* but also throughout the rest of her fiction may very well have sprung from this source. Or perhaps her belief in such relationships was reinforced by her friendship with Frede, whom she came to know better as they both entered young womanhood. It was the glorious talk, the struggle toward an understanding of the world and its inhabitants, combined with the expression of various epiphanies, that gave the relationship its flavour—that and a shared youth, rife with family lore, on the island. For ancestry, and the variety of ancestor worship that is rooted in place, would necessarily have played a significant role in the bond between them.

Frederica Campbell was the youngest of four children born to Maud's Aunt Anna (Macneill) and Uncle John Campbell of the much-loved farm in Park Corner, Prince Edward Island. In Montgomery's early diaries, there are several accounts of jolly times at Park Corner, mostly in the company of the older girl cousins, Stella and Clara. After the strictures set in place by her Macneill grandparents, a visit to the tumultuous, vibrant world of the house in Park Corner, with four young people there to welcome her, must have been a breath of fresh air, and more than once the young Maud gives accounts of raucous, uncontrollable laughter brought on by a variety of hijinks. "I'm nearly half dead from laughing," she wrote during a February 1892 visit. "Clara and I talked most of the night last night. When the girls came home from school we began to make and eat pancakes and we laughed until the pancakes nearly choked us. My head is splitting from the racket. It is all very foolish I suppose but it is a delightful foolishness."

Delightful indeed. The more we come to know about the loneliness of Montgomery's youth as well as the difficulties of her later life, the more we are grateful for such "foolish" interludes in her childhood and young womanhood. The kind of unbridled, almost hysterical, laughter that is a part of any girlhood would have been rare in Maud's grandparents' house. But the busy, expansive world of Park Corner allowed for a variety of experiences to unfold without interference from adults.

Probably because of the nine-year gap in their ages, a gap that would seem to narrow once they were both adults, Frede does not make a significant appearance in the journals until a number of years later, in early spring of 1910. Maud had been looking after her widowed grandmother in Cavendish for some time, and it was a subdued Montgomery who wrote the entry describing her cousin's visit:

> Frede Campbell came up from Cape Traverse— where she is teaching—on Tuesday to spend Easter with me. I believe that all I need is companionship. I felt like a different being when she was here. We talked out all our difficulties and worries and they did not loom so blackly and menacingly when put into words. I feel strengthened and able to go on. I think if Frede had not come to see me I must have given up completely. What a great blessing faithful friendship is—the friendship of a true woman on whom one can depend and in whom one can trust.

They had become close a few years previously, when Maud was twenty-eight and Frede nineteen. During one of Maud's visits to Park Corner, they discovered quite suddenly that they shared similar world views and, even more important, they both were starved for conversation. They had talked all night about their inner lives and most especially about their loves. Both had suffered disappointments in this arena (though it could be said of Maud that, unlike Frede, she disappointed men more than she was disappointed by them), and they found they were able to confess many things to each other without judging and without being judged. Montgomery, in those days, was a passionate talker, and on several occasions she had talked all night with one female chum or another. But with Frede it was more like a communion than a simple discussion. Frede was a remarkably bright and ambitious young woman, and as cousins Frede and Maud had in common a pantheon of relatives whose domestic dramas were acted out in intimately familiar settings. It should also be remembered that Maud had no siblings. Frede, therefore, and to a lesser extent her older sister Stella, were like sisters to Maud, providing her with a variety of family permanence and security. Stella, in later life, would also provide Maud with the kind of irritation that has been known to accompany the joys of sisterhood, but if we are to believe the diaries not a single shadow entered the relationship with Frede, and the friendship between the two women deepened with each encounter.

Frede was not only a night talker, she was useful as well, and almost always on hand for the significant milestones of Montgomery's life. She was at Maud's wedding, for example, and was there to see Maud model her trousseau beforehand. She was also present at the birth of baby Chester, Montgomery's first child (her second, Hugh, died in infancy, and her third, Stuart, was born about a year later), and was in the vicinity when Chester graduated from wearing long dresses and was put into short pants. A good deal of lightheartedness accompanied childrearing sessions when Frede was on the premises, as evidenced by the delightful poem the two women concocted concerning Frede and Punch (baby Chester's nickname):

There was a pirate known as Wag
Whose Sunday name was Punch
He sailed upon the raging main
And ate his aunts for lunch

He liked them fricasseed and stewed
But sometimes for a change
He broiled them nice and tenderly
Upon his kitchen range

And when an aunt was saucier
Than usual Waggy said
"I'll have you made into a hash
You gristly old Aunt Frede."

> But when Aunt Stella was served up
> Wag wouldn't touch a bite
> He said, "If I et her I'd have
> Most awful dreams tonight."

The joy and intimacy of Frede's visits was almost always followed by sadness at her departure, indicating how lonely Montgomery really was, and how isolated, both by her position as minister's wife and by her fame as an author. Neither of these personae allowed for any real friendships with neighbours, particularly if they were parishioners. She had not developed close associations in the literary world, and the friends of her girlhood for the most part remained in Prince Edward Island. How valuable the connection with Frede must have been, with its combination of family ties and true comradeship. Moreover, around 1911 Frede, also an exile from Prince Edward Island, had been nearby, studying at Macdonald College of Home Economics in Montreal. When, after graduation and a lengthy stay with Maud, Frede left to take a position at the Ladies College in Red Deer, Alberta, Montgomery was filled with melancholy. "It seems so horribly far away," she wrote in her diary:

> We have never been so far separated before. It makes me wretched to think of it. I shall miss her

so horribly—our little chats, our little jokes, our
delightful eye-to-eye vision of everything, our
sympathy with and understanding of one another.

Frede stayed in the West for a year and then, to Maud's
delight, in 1913 decided to return to the eastern provinces,
where she eventually took up a position at Macdonald
College. Thanks to the railway, she was able to visit Maud's
home during this period a couple of times a year. In 1915, on
a journey back to Prince Edward Island, Montgomery parted
from Frede (who had been visiting) en route, in Montreal.
"I looked back as we hastened to our train," she wrote, "and
saw her standing, a lonely figure in the crowded station." "If
Frede and I could only see each other oftener," she added, "it
seems to me that I would ask nothing else of life."

One can visualize Maud on the remainder of that journey, sitting on the train with a husband she admittedly did
not love, longing for the simple companionship her cousin
provided. There would be little conversation beyond the
necessary details of the trip and various ministrations concerning the now three-year-old Chester, for Ewan does not
appear to have been a communicator. Maud on the other
hand would have wanted the running commentary, the
shared observations and thoughts that a good friend gives
and receives. When Frede was not there, the diary took her

place. And it was in the diary that Maud poured out her heart about what became of her "bosom friend."

The war years were very difficult for Montgomery. A sensitive soul and an alarmist by nature, she felt deeply the great losses suffered by those around her and harboured an authentic, almost paranoid dread about the state of the world in general. A number of personal tragedies further darkened her life. At the beginning of the war, in August 1914, her son Hugh, "little Hugh," as she came to call him, was born dead as a result of a problem with the umbilical cord. Maud was devastated and became nervous and depressed until, in October 1915, she gave birth to another, this time healthy, baby boy named Stuart. But Maud had her own physical problems: a chronic infection in her breast and attacks of sleeplessness. At one point, in 1916, she weighed only 109 pounds. "This war is slowly killing me," she wrote. "I am bleeding to death as France is being bled in the shambles of Verdun." Though she and Ewan shared the details of the war, it was only during Frede's visits that Maud was able to express her full horror and her indignation, her secret terror. "When has a New Year dawned, freighted by such awful possibilities?" she asked her diary on January 1, 1915, then confessed, "I am very lonely tonight. Frede left today on her return to Macdonald."

Even Frede herself became a temporary source of anxiety. In April 1915 Maud was called to her bedside in Montreal when Frede almost died of typhoid fever. She recovered from the illness, however, and was able to join a pregnant Maud at Park Corner in July of that year. They revisited familiar haunts and in the evening walked back and forth over the old bridge, listening to the roar of the surf on the nearby shore until "twilight suddenly was night and the shining new moon swung above the treetops that bend over that old homestead." Then, a year and a half later, Frede stunned Montgomery by suddenly marrying Lieutenant Cameron MacFarlane—a man eight years her junior—two days before his return to the front. Maud was not necessarily pleased by the match and was somewhat hurt as well that she had not been told about their wedding. This oversight was happily cleared up when she discovered that Frede had sent a telegram, which had never arrived. The friendship blossomed as always, and the two women went shopping, attended a couple of teas, heard British foreign minister Arthur Balfour speak at the Royal Victoria College, and spent the nights "thrashing over" Frede's problems. "We laughed so much during the process," Montgomery confessed, "that we did not make any great headway in solving them." Many more delightful visits would follow, as

MacFarlane was conveniently away with his regiment, though no farther than New Brunswick, which was likely not as distant as Montgomery would have liked. When she finally met him, she found him shallow and limited in the extreme.

Not quite two years later, while her husband was still away in service, Frede was once again taken ill, this time with the brutal Spanish influenza that was ravaging most of the western world. Once again Montgomery rushed to her friend's bedside, but this time the trip was even more frantic. Maud had been in Boston attending to legal problems with her publisher L.C. Page when news reached her that Frede, whom she had been intending to visit in Montreal on her return, had come down with the flu. At first she was not overly concerned, knowing that Frede was receiving good care, but a further message and a couple of her portentous dreams greatly increased her anxiety. When she arrived at the infirmary of Macdonald College, she believed that her friend would be dead. Frede was still alive but had contracted pneumonia, and all concerned, Montgomery included, knew it would be only a matter of time. Three days later, at dawn on January 20, 1919, Maud's dearest friend died.

Montgomery's reaction was extreme. She left the deathbed, entered a nearby empty room, and found herself consumed by uncontrollable, hysterical laughter, which continued until one of the nurses gave her either a stimulant or a sedative—she was never quite sure which—whereupon she collapsed into a deep sleep. This was followed by two days of pacing. "All that day I walked the floor of the beautiful living room—all the next interminable day I walked it," she wrote later in her journal. Tears eventually came, but they brought no comfort. And apart from Miss Hill and Miss Kirby, staff members at Macdonald College, she was on her own and responsible for all decisions, from what Frede should wear in her coffin to whether she should be cremated. She attended the cremation alone, and alone, with occasional help from Frede's sister-in-law, who would have been a stranger to Maud, she sorted the few possessions Frede had left behind in her rooms.

Exhausted by sorrow, Maud returned to Leaskdale, to a husband who would shortly succumb once more to mental instability and to children who would soon begin to disappoint her. She never recovered from the trauma of losing Frede, the only person who knew and understood the many facets of her complicated personality. Each year, on the anniversary of Frede's death, Maud would feel the anguish as keenly as ever. Subsequent visits to Prince Edward Island, and especially to Park Corner, would be particularly painful, bringing to mind lost youth as well as lost friendship. Shortly after returning from that harrowing winter trip to Macdonald College, Maud pasted the photo of the dark iron gates that gave entrance to the institution's grounds. Covered in ice and surrounded by snow, they look not unlike gates to the underworld. Montgomery did not explain her inclusion of this image in her diary, the only confidante she now possessed. Instead, she wrote:

> Well, it is all over. It has been my privilege to possess for seventeen years a rare and perfect friendship—something that is very rare in this world, especially between women. Perhaps some day I may be thankful that I had it even at the cost of losing it. Just now the agony seems too great a price to pay.

CHAPTER SIX

Places

Almost every title of Montgomery's twenty books contains the name of a place. *The Story Girl*, *A Tangled Web*, *Mistress Pat*, and *Magic for Marigold* are the exceptions, along with *Emily Climbs* and *Emily's Quest*, although we are well aware that the Emily in question is the heroine of *Emily of New Moon*, the first book of that trilogy. The places named in the titles are essential to the texture of Montgomery's work. Not only does rural landscape and architecture act as a mirror to various facets of characters' individuality in the novels, but the details of geography are closely observed and described by the author. Anne, in a bourgeois city house, or Emily, in a girls' boarding school—both would have necessarily been girls without a pastoral view. It is essential to these fictional young women that they become able to choose, and then name, favourite roads, fields, houses, woods, ponds, and vistas. Anne, the orphan, gets down to the business of naming, and therefore in some way possessing, various features of the landscape immediately upon arrival in the vicinity of Avonlea, much to the amazement of Matthew, who drives her from the station to Green Gables. The Avenue and Barry's Pond are transformed by the child into White Way of Delight and the Lake of Shining Waters, almost as if she had changed the topography simply by looking at it. Similarly, Bev and Felix in *The Story Girl* and Jane in *Jane of Lantern Hill* come fully alive only after they have left urban life behind and entered a rural terrain where they feel free to name and mythologize the phenomena of the natural and, to a somewhat lesser extent, the built world around them. Places are cherished, almost worshipped—for this is a variety of pantheism—and once they have attained their sacred status, certain features of the landscape are revisited so often that the world achieves reassuring stability. Nothing in the landscape will ever change.

Montgomery was greatly attached to places, those associated with her childhood on the island in particular, but also the geographical surroundings and enclosed spaces of the various houses she occupied in her adult life. She didn't have to be wildly happy in a place for its singularity to have power over her, but the fleeting and the casual could never hold her. To form the required emotional connection with a place, she needed to walk the roads, climb the hills, live for several seasons in the rooms. Then they became like family to her, perhaps the only family—apart from Frede and her cats—she could count on.

The places she loved appeared in various disguises in the novels, but they were also much documented in her journals and the vast number of photographs she took all through her life. Montgomery was a record keeper, a chronicler of reality as well as a creator of fantasy. Words and photographs could freeze the world, protect it from mutability, and she wrote about and photographed her island home, and later Leaskdale and Norval, extensively. There is something both tender and touching about her attention to the smallest details, her photographs of her girlhood room on the Macneill farm (her "own dear den," as she called it), or the country road the boys took to school near Leaskdale, or the one she herself had taken to Cavendish school. She photographed and wrote about her cats, her furniture, views from windows, fences, back lanes, significant verandas, gardens, everyone she loved, and even people, like Isobel, whom she did not. Her early scrapbooks were a testament both to time and to place and, again an effort to make things hold still, to preserve splinters from the woodwork of beloved houses, corsages worn on pleasant evenings, fabric from admired dresses, programs from performances and festivities, and the dust jackets of her own books so that they would not disintegrate and vanish from her life.

Houses were terribly important to her, beginning with the old Macneill farm, where she spent her childhood. It was a plain frame building, and very little human warmth was given to her inside its walls, but Montgomery held the simple farmhouse close to her heart all her life, often pasting photographs of its rooms in her diary years after she had left it behind. She added on one occasion a caption beneath a small panorama of the Macneill farm that read, "Home as it was Long Years Ago."

Some of the most heart-rending passages in the journals relate to her revisiting her old home years after her grandmother's death. These journeys into the past would take place during summer visits to Prince Edward Island and were made doubly poignant by the fact that after her uncle John Macneill inherited the farm, he had left the house vacant. In 1913, two years after she had left the island when she married, Montgomery once again stood on Laird's Hill and looked down at the homestead. "I stood there long," she wrote later,

> and never have I felt keener pangs, never did my heart ache more bitterly with longing and a sense of loss. And as I stood there I thought—not of home empty and forsaken—not of home as it was in the years before I left it—but of home as it was long years ago.

In her mind she conjured everything that had been familiar to her as a child—a form of self-torture really—which caused her to weep, then she walked up to the gate at the end of the lane, where she was horrified to discover not a drive leading to the yard, but a field of potatoes. She knew then that with the disappearance of the lane, which she had considered to be "as much a part of the landscape as the hills or woods," it was no good venturing farther; her entrance "to the past was closed—it was gone altogether." She turned and walked away, the spectre of homelessness, a ghost that had haunted her since her mother's death and her father's departure, once again at her side.

Against her better judgment she eventually went back, once in 1918 and then again some years later. On the 1918 visit she actually approached the door of her old room but found that she could not make herself enter. A few years later, the yard was completely overgrown, the clapboard walls unpainted. (As always, Montgomery took a photograph, which she pasted in her journal near another photo showing the house in its prime.) Though the house had been empty almost a decade, the furniture was still in place, as if waiting for the old inhabitants to dust it off and resume the life that had been lived there. She did not linger for long and, uncharacteristically, did not report her emotions at any great length in her diary: "I felt sad—sad—sad. I seemed a ghost among ghosts. I was glad to get away. And I shall never be there again."

Park Corner, however, stayed more or less as she had known it, due in part to the kind of financial help Montgomery offered the members of the family who remained there. This had been a happy house for Maud, and early on she had photographed its rooms with the kind of enthusiasm that suggests some joyful incident or another had taken place in each recorded corner. It is significant, for example, that she chose to take a picture of the pantry, the site of many daytime and nighttime raids by her and Frede. In the interval between her grandmother's death and her marriage to Ewan, a period of two or three months, Maud had remained at Park Corner, and despite missing her old home in Cavendish, she photographed the exterior of the house, put an *X* beside the window of the room she had occupied, and then photographed the interior of that room, as if to make solid her notion that Park Corner was, and always would be, her "second home." It was in this second home that she was married, on July 5, 1911, "standing before the mantel" in the parlour, which she also photographed. It was while sitting beside her new husband at her bridal banquet in the house that Maud experienced a prescient sense of despair.

"I felt a sudden horrible inrush of *rebellion* and *despair*," she wrote, making use of the infamous italics. "*I wanted to be free!* I felt like a prisoner—a hopeless prisoner. . . . I sat at that gay bridal feast, in my white veil and orange blossoms, beside the man I had married—and I was as unhappy as I had ever been in my life." Potent emotions: ones that were not easy to override, especially since they took place in rooms that, in the past, had provided an escape from negativity. Yet override them she did, venturing forth from Park Corner and into married life.

She would return to Park Corner on summer holidays with her two boys in tow, and sometimes with Ewan and Frede. Often the house was overflowing with children, and mealtimes would become especially chaotic. Montgomery would later recall that on one of these occasions Frede had been the thirteenth to sit at the table. Always superstitious and a believer in portents, she would recall with shame how she had leaned toward her friend and jokingly said, "No use getting up now—your doom is sealed. May as well sit down and eat resignedly."

But even Park Corner was not exempt from change. Some of the old people who had brightened Maud's childhood would die, and their places would be filled by youngsters whose manners Maud did not always like. And even though in the earlier visits she was happily in the company of Frede ("I can't conceive of Frede and I foregathering, even at seventy, and not being able to laugh," she wrote), she mourned the farm she had known as a youngster. Financial difficulty, for the first time since the farm was cleared a century before, had made itself known, and George Campbell, the only son, had proved to be neither industrious nor reliable. "The Park Corner of today," she declared in her diary, "still beautiful, still almost the same outwardly, is a terribly different place from the Park Corner of twenty years ago. And I am not sorry that I go tomorrow."

Being a revenant by nature, Montgomery would come back to Park Corner several times throughout her life: in 1921 in the company of a morose and self-absorbed Ewan, who was experiencing "that wretched obsession of guilt and punishment," and in 1923 when once again she found the spectre of change waiting for her on the island. Her Uncle John had finally pulled down the "old house" in Cavendish, and when she arrived at Park Corner, she found her Aunt Annie thin and gaunt, having "failed" somewhat since her last visit. She returned again in July 1924 for her aunt's funeral. "There have been eight funerals in that house," she stated, "and only one wedding—mine." The loss of so many, and particularly of Frede and Aunt Annie, both such positive figures (the former as a sister and best friend, the latter as a surrogate mother), must have been sharply felt by Maud whenever she returned. When she visited in 1927, and again in 1929, she was beset by phantoms. Once, during the latter visit, she found herself alone in the parlour. "I was suddenly overwhelmed with agony," she wrote, "so keen I could only endure it by walking up and down. I spent an hour there with my ghosts." Later her mood had evidently brightened, and she reported she was much amused to find a regular war had broken out between Cavendish and Park Corner, each hamlet insisting that its pond was the prototype for the fictional Anne Shirley's Lake of Shining Waters.

By the time of her 1929 visit, Maud had truly begun to lose hope about the future of Park Corner. In spite of her frequent financial donations, she felt the house, outbuildings, fields, and orchards were not being cared for and that the whole property had an "unlived" look. By 1932 things had reached an impasse. The livestock had been sold and the land rented out; there was talk of selling the farm outright. Aunt Annie had bequeathed Park Corner to her son Dan, but he, not inclined to be a farmer, had decamped to Los Angeles. A younger brother, Jim, seemed more interested, but Dan could not be persuaded to hand over the farm ownership. The relatives wanted Maud to intervene not only with more money, but also to convince Dan to give the farm up.

At first she hesitated. So much time, effort, and money had already gone into Park Corner that she was beginning to run out of energy. "Moreover," she wrote, "I have—I admit it—grown *superstitious* about any place I love or try to help. I seem to bring it bad luck. It never prospers no matter what is done." She must have been thinking of her childhood home, abandoned, and eventually demolished, or perhaps her birthplace, the house in which her mother died. In the end she wrote to Dan—a practical, no-nonsense kind of letter—and finally he decided to give the farm over to Jim.

It was during this particular bout of uncertainty about Park Corner that Maud, with some difficulty, began to write *Pat of Silver Bush*. She had been feeling unwell, was suffering from headaches, depression, and sleeplessness, and was often anxious about Ewan's mental state or the boys' examination results or both. In her journals she admitted she was finding the writing difficult. And yet *Pat* proved to be another of her joyful creations, one in which home and a known and loved landscape were dominant themes. The physical characteristics and temperament of Pat herself cannot help but make the reader think of Frede and, by extension, of Pat's farm as Park Corner. Pat's insistence that Silver Bush should never change puts one in mind of Maud's own attempts to keep her beloved second home intact.

In February 1935, when Maud and her husband left the Norval manse in order to move to Toronto, she began her packing in the attic. "I had loved my garret so," she wrote. "I always loved garrets—I suppose because of the fun long ago in the old Park Corner garret." She goes on to describe the view from the windows, then adds: "I worked till dark then broke down. I felt as if my heart were actually broken." Her last two diary entries concerning Park Corner were written in 1937 and 1938. The first included copies of the "ten year" letters she and Frede had written to each other in 1907 to be opened in 1917. The second concerned some photos of the old farm, which had been mailed to Maud. There was one view of the house. "It shows," Maud wrote, "as I had not realized, how the trees have grown up around it, since I took my last snap of it twenty-seven years ago." Something about the simplicity of this statement makes it more moving than the many detailed descriptions of time and loss included elsewhere in the journals.

Eventually Montgomery's much-loved places were subjected to the kind of "preservation" that guaranteed the very change Montgomery dreaded. Not long after *Anne of Green Gables* was published in 1911, tourists searching for

Green Gables began arriving in Prince Edward Island in the vicinity of Cavendish. Soon a rumour began to circulate suggesting that the house owned by Montgomery's cousin Pierce Macneill (and later by Ernest Webb) was the prototype for Green Gables. Montgomery partially corroborated this rumour in a diary entry dated January 27, 1911, but added it was "not so much the house itself as the situations and the scenery" that had inspired her. On a trip to the island a decade later, Maud noticed with wry amusement that the government had erected signs pointing visitors toward the site of Green Gables, but she noted in her diary that she was happy that the Webbs, who were by then in possession of the property, were able to make a tidy sum from the tea shop they had established on the premises. In 1936, however, Maud was very concerned when she heard that "the Gov't is going to purchase a site for a national park and it is possible that the Webb farm will be bought for it—or part of it. Because of *Anne* forsooth!! The thought is a terrible one to me. What change and heartache may it not mean!" "And yet," she adds gloomily, "when I love a place, is it not doomed?"

Once the Prince Edward Island National Park was established, battalions of tourists began arriving from all over the world. In the last decade, for example, six thousand Japanese tourists a year have made the trip to "Green Gables," and that is only 3 percent of the total number of visitors. Gift shops, tea shops, hotels, and a Green Gables Golf Course would appear. (The golf course surrounds the Macneill-Webb house, now a museum, whose gables are kept freshly painted and as green as the considerable number of American dollars spent in the vicinity.) Musicals would be written and performed, and television dramas and their spinoffs would be developed and aired. Anne dolls would be mass-produced, cookbooks would be published, bed and breakfast establishments would proliferate, and theme parks would open. Anniversaries of the first publication of *Anne of Green Gables* would be celebrated and much publicized. There are even carrot-red Anne wigs available in the plethora of gift shops in and around Cavendish, for those tourists feeling lighthearted enough to wear them.

Many jobs have been created on the island, jobs that give local students the summer employment they need to continue their education and that allow some of the province's families who might have migrated elsewhere to remain in the land of their forefathers. But for an author—or any human being, for that matter—to witness her own private, inspirational landscape, one that is both an outer and inner geography, both real and imagined, being marketed to such a degree can only be confusing and painful. Montgomery did not live long enough to see the extent of the industry that would develop around the places she loved. But in 1937, five years before her death, she would enter two short sentences in her diary concerning what was unfolding in the Cavendish area. "There are bitter quarrels," she wrote, "going on down there over the Park business. I wish it had never been heard of, after all." It is unclear whether she wished the park, the Cavendish area, or her own writing had never been heard of. Perhaps she was able to keep her own version of that landscape somewhere in her mind and heart, but in her journals she never mentioned the park again.

CHAPTER SEVEN

The Work

In her later life, Lucy Maud Montgomery developed asthma. She would describe the feeling of suffocation that accompanied the cough, the sense that she would never again catch her breath, her fear that she would end up "a wheezing nuisance." What caused these spells was never clear, not to her, and not to the future readers of her diaries. Knowing what we now know, however, about the connection between asthma—a condition that acts as a perfect metaphor for suppressed emotions—and the state of mind of its victims, it is almost surprising that the disease did not develop sooner in Maud's life. Suppression, it would seem, became part of her daily life very early on, and even after she became a world-famous author she was never free for long from a feeling of entrapment and suffocation.

During the eight-year period Maud was required to take care of her grandmother, references to depression begin to appear in the diaries, often coupled with descriptions of miserable weather that confined her to her quarters. She is snowbound. She is storm-stayed. The much-longed-for mail can't get through to the kitchen post office. No one can get in and she can't get out. The rooms of the house are dimmed by the drifts crawling up the windows and blocking out the light. Her thrifty Presbyterian grandmother will allow only so much coal oil for the lamps and scant fuel for the fire. It is cold and dark and there is no conversation beyond that needed to run a household. In January 1907, Montgomery writes:

> I wonder if, sometime in the future, I shall ever again find Sunday evenings pleasant. For the past six years they have, for the most part—in winter at least—epitomized for me all that was dreary and lusterless in my existence.

In February, she adds:

> We have had "a dreadful cold spell"—five days away below zero. The house has got so cold that it is really not fit to live in, as grandmother will not have a fire anywhere but in the kitchen. . . . This is the most utterly, lonely winter I have ever put in. . . . Day after day drags by, cold, lifeless, monotonous.

And yet during the long winters of 1905, 1906, and 1907, and especially through the spring, summer, and fall, there were some good times. She developed a close bond with a local schoolteacher, Norah Lefurgey, who boarded at her grandmother's, and her intense friendship with Frede became a sustaining force. Both young women were referred to with joy in her diaries. With them, in the milder seasons, she could share the walks through the fields and lanes and along the beaches that delighted her. She took some wonderful pictures of Norah on Cavendish Beach and Frede emerging from a stand of birches or laughing in the kitchen.

What Maud scarcely mentions in her diaries during those years is the fact that a young, single man of the cloth named Ewan Macdonald had in 1903 become the new minister at the Cavendish church, and that in 1906, before he departed for further training in Glasgow, Scotland, she had secretly accepted his proposal of marriage. This seems odd when before this her diaries were filled with the ups and downs of her relationships with young men: the boys who had been attracted to her during her teens, her engagement (and her breaking of same) to her cousin Edwin Simpson, her painful affair with Herman Leard. And yet now that an apparently appropriate suitor was on the threshold, Montgomery, who must have known what Ewan's visits would lead to, decided not to record her feelings, or not to any great extent.

A remarkable kind of revisionist history was unfolding in Maud's imagination and on the page, if not on the pages of her journals: a history, or more accurately a fiction, that would turn out to be both the result of and in direct opposition to the circumstances of her own childhood. The work she was doing while tending to her grandmother's needs during the old woman's last illness, and during her long engagement to Ewan Macdonald, would not only make her famous, but would serve as a template for many more fictions to come. The idea of an elderly couple applying to an orphan asylum for a hired boy and receiving a girl by mistake had come to her as a narrative she might use as a story for a "certain Sunday School paper," but the character of the girl in question had captivated her creator to such an extent that she "cast 'moral' and 'Sunday School' ideals to the winds," and Anne became "a real human girl."

As Irene Gammel has brought to our attention in her absorbing book *Looking for Anne: How Lucy Maud Montgomery Dreamed Up a Literary Classic*, a widely divergent and plentiful selection of ingredients went into this work of alchemy: fantasy, childhood experiences, romanticism, anger, humour, sentimentality, and loss were all mixed into the brew. Added to this were Montgomery's own enthusiasm for and engagement with her subject.

"Nothing I have ever written gave me so much pleasure to write," she told her journal. "Many of my own childhood experiences and dreams were worked up into its chapters." The phrase "worked up into its chapters" tells us that during the winter when she worked on *Anne* a miraculous transformation from recalled experience to work of art had taken place, and, as Montgomery says, the narrative became dependent not just on a setting or an accumulation of incidents, but also on the character of the fictional Anne herself. *"She* is the book," Montgomery declared.

Still, as she also confided, a great deal of the child that Lucy Maud Montgomery once was went into the development of this character as well: her rebelliousness in the face of insensitive, judgmental adults, for example, or even something as simple as a general sense of abandonment and isolation combined with a nagging desire to please (and therefore to be loved), which is constantly in the background as the narrative progresses. The reader sees Anne becoming affectionate with the adults who have offended and hurt her, and sees, as well, the same adults softening under the spell of her eccentric charm. Under the curbing influence of societal pressures, her extreme imagination becomes more private and withdrawn and, as a result, perhaps more powerful. Maud herself wanted desperately to be accepted by the very conservative family and society into which she was born, and therefore kept her romantic, imaginative side a secret from her elder relatives and sometimes even from herself.

In the years to come, as evidenced by the content of her journals, she would also keep the two very different kinds of writing separate, only now and then allowing one to inform the other in any obvious way. Occasionally, the description of a place from the journal will enter the setting of a book, or the diary will comment on an achievement or a setback in her career, but with the exception of one long, faintly self-conscious passage chronicling the development of *Anne of Green Gables* written well after the fact with— one suspects—posterity on her mind, there is very little talk in Maud's journals about the process of writing, and even less about how her imagination chose a subject, a character, a tone. These things she kept close to her heart or quite possibly prevented them from coming fully to consciousness at all. For Lucy Maud Montgomery, the place where the imagination rearranged episodes from a painful childhood was one best visited by an oblique, almost evasive route—for the sake of the transformation demanded by her art, but also for the sake of her psyche, which needed to heal— however inadequately—the wounds of her youth rather than reopen them.

It is interesting to speculate what might have happened on the page if Montgomery had gone into those dark spaces with her eyes wide open. Would her fiction have been more brutally honest, her characters more psychologically driven? She claimed in her journal not to admire the realist writing of Canadian Morley Callaghan, preferring to avoid all that she considered "ugly" in the realm of human relationships. And yet she read George Eliot with pleasure, a writer whose psychological analysis of character is strikingly direct. And she read and appreciated Emily Brontë's *Wuthering Heights*, a book in which the Romantic and Gothic become authentically disturbing, and therefore more powerful, when viewed against the backdrop of character, class, and geography.

I have a friend with whom I have often talked about Montgomery's life and work. She is a writer of fiction who, like Montgomery, was brought up as a Presbyterian in a Canadian rural setting. Often we get together for very long lunches, during which we talk about almost everything, except politics. We like to think of ourselves as intellectuals of a sort, but we are given nevertheless to a great deal of speculation concerning the mysteries of human nature. A lot of the time we talk about what it is like to be a woman writer living not in the thick of the book world, but on the ragged edges of that world: close enough to participate if we want to but far enough away for complete withdrawal if we prefer that. We talk about that choice, because for us it is a choice, but we have also discussed what it must have been like for our forebears in this country, women who for any number of reasons—social, economic, religious, familial—would not have had much choice at all. So far, we have not been able to decide whether Montgomery falls into the latter category, whether she was one without choice, but we lean toward the notion that she does. For all we know, however, Montgomery—even had she felt free to do whatever she wanted—might very well have chosen her role as a dutiful caretaker of an aged grandmother, followed by a life in which the obligations of a minister's wife were accepted without question.

My friend and I have recited those obligations aloud to each other. Bake sales, we have said. Visits with the elderly and infirm. Teas with the wives of church elders. Rummage sales. Christmas bazaars. Funerals. Weddings. Listening to husband's sermons. Listening to husband's rants. Care and feeding of visiting ministers. Teaching Sunday school. Wearing the appropriate clothing, hats, footwear, hairstyle, facial expression. And likely, we eventually concluded, publishing the appropriate fiction.

Certainly, the charming domestic world Lucy Maud Montgomery presents to us in her fiction is a reflection of almost all the facets of her actual life, or at least the public surface of her actual life. (What went on beneath that surface has been proven, with the publication of her diaries, to be much more unsettling than anyone could have guessed.) Her protagonists, in spite of their high spirits, eccentricities, cleverness, ambition, and creative tendencies, are driven by loyalty to the friends and families of the rural world from which they come and are delighted by the natural beauty of their own particular place. This devotion and delight runs like a sparkling stream through all the books and enhances our enjoyment as we read.

But my friend insists that Montgomery was holding back, that had she given herself permission to do so she could have written adult fiction as compelling as that of Charlotte Brontë or George Eliot—both of whom, Montgomery confesses in her diaries, she "may have dreamed of rivaling" in her "salad days"—or of her American contemporaries Edith Wharton or Willa Cather. But how would such cerebral and possibly sexual drama be received in the conservative Protestant society Montgomery lived in and wrote about? Half a century before Montgomery was writing, the Brontës avoided the scorn of their own particular Protestant community by adopting male pseudonyms. In her personal life George Eliot escaped the bonds of Victorian social order but nevertheless also felt compelled to adopt a male pseudonym. This suggests that even after Eliot had eschewed convention, she felt that the act of scrutinizing on paper the storms of human passion and vagaries of human behaviour was better accepted if done by a man.

How to explain the Americans, the Cathers and Whartons, who appeared in print just a few decades after Eliot and who were unafraid to put their own names to narratives that lean toward the dark? In the case of Edith Wharton, wealth may have offered a kind of intellectual freedom or at least a buffer. Being born as she was in New York, at the very top of the social ladder, she had access, even as a girl, to educational, cultural, and social experiences almost unheard of in Prince Edward Island. The rural world of Willa Cather's childhood was similar to that of Montgomery's, but Cather's involvement in sexual friendships with women, rather than men, meant that her path through adulthood would have followed a route very different from that taken by a bright young heterosexual woman interested in literature yet wanting acceptance in the sphere of ordinary domesticity. Perhaps Montgomery would not have wanted ordinary domesticity to such a degree had the domestic life of her own childhood been more secure. And if her mother had lived, for example, or if her father had not removed himself from her life, she might not have felt compelled to create narratives in which, over and over again, an unhappy orphan, or semi-orphan, or the daughter of separated parents is able—often as a result of the charm that emanates from her own rich personality—to win over the stern adults who have taken on the task of raising her so that they come to cherish her and provide her with a happy childhood. This is true of the famous Anne, but also of Emily (of New Moon) and Jane (of Lantern Hill), and determines the prototype for Sara Stanley in *The Story Girl* as well.

The need to romanticize her surroundings—in short, to make things seem better, more beautiful, and, most important, safer than they were—was always with Montgomery, my friend and I decided. Both of us had visited Leaskdale, Ontario, where Ewan and Maud made their first home in the manse and where Ewan preached in the Presbyterian church. It was mysteriously grim there, we concluded, and grim without reason. The south view of hills descending step by step like a giant's staircase toward Lake Ontario, the north view of the solid and not altogether unattractive brick church, and the east and west views of rustic, rail-fenced fields should have made a pleasant prospect, but somehow it didn't. The wind felt cruel, even though we had both been there in summer, and in the arid bareness nothing flourished. *Empty* and *stark* were the adjectives we found ourselves using to describe the village. It had the look of a place where things had gone bad, and would continue to go bad for anyone foolish enough to settle there. The official blue metal plaque announcing Montgomery's association with the spot was the same as those one sees here and there all over the province of Ontario commemorating battles.

And yet Montgomery grieved when she left the Leaskdale manse for the far more charming valley that contained the village of Norval. Her boys were born in Leaskdale, she tells us in her diary, were small children there, and had slept peacefully in the manse through many a winter storm. (She neglects at this point to mention the storms that occurred *inside* the manse.) She had made a garden there, reared beloved pets, and her cherished Frede had visited those rooms. Maud probably wanted to cram the whole place into her scrapbook, or would have wanted to, had her scrapbooks not begun to change by then. She could keep the darkness out of almost everything else: her demeanour, her duties, her fiction. But there were two places where it couldn't be brushed aside. Her scrapbooks became, at least partially, a chronicle of bad news: shipwrecks, battles, and other tragedies, where once there had been bouquets, decals, and locks of loved ones' hair. And her diaries: it was through her diaries that we learn not only about life's petty and not-so-petty complaints, about lost and broken heirlooms and less than helpful maids, but also about her grief, her worry and disappointment, and about Ewan and his disorder.

There was certainly a precedent for the body of socially acceptable writing to which Montgomery, in her fiction, may have felt she was contributing. One has only to think of the seed catalogues and the women's magazines that first published the work of her fictional echo Emily Starr, or the Sunday school paper for which Maud herself first conceived the idea of Anne. In fact, self-expression—especially for girls—was encouraged within the conservative social order as long as that expression did not stray from a formulaic, sentimental rendition of that which was perceived to be feminine, and as long as it chronicled the triumphs of various virtues or rhapsodized about the beauty of nature. Moreover, the "literary club," or "the literary" as Maud refers to it in her diaries, was a staple of small-town social life. In *Canadian Crystals*, a volume of self-published verse that appeared at the turn of the twentieth century, Reverend Thomas Watson, who lived and preached in rural Ontario, penned a poem for just such a gathering.

> To understand Canadian thought
> Observing well each polished gem
> To learn of minds who bravely fought
> For precious truths most dear to them
> To blend instruction with delight
> These are the objects which unite
> The literary club.

"Thank God," Maud wrote in an autumn diary entry in 1908, a couple of years before her marriage, "I can keep the shadows of my life out of my work." But did she really? The orphans and semi-orphans she so often focused on were a serious social problem of the time, and the small towns in which these young people tried to make their way were at times rendered by Montgomery as conservative and against the imagination. Though presented in an engaging and ultimately winning manner, the anguish of the child who does not feel loved is present in many of the books, as is the hardship encountered by talented young women who are trying to live a creative life. This may not be full shade, but Montgomery's work is not by any means all about sunlight either; her use of chiaroscuro creates, I would argue, a complete and meaningful canvas. Marginalized individuals, often those troubled by mental disorders, are sympathetically but accurately depicted, as are those suffering from poverty. Tragedy often enters the narrative and sometimes in genuinely disturbing ways, especially in the Emily trilogy. Montgomery may have allowed a brilliant light to illuminate the scenes, but it was one that exposed rather than concealed. Only some of the darker shadows, therefore, are never eliminated.

But the shadows she felt she was banishing from her fiction at that early stage of her life and writing career were not so terribly threatening. At the time, and in spite of long, dreary winters rife with cabin fever, Maud was still mostly an optimistic and enthusiastic young woman, delighted with her own unimaginable success, enjoying the company of her female friends, and looking forward to the companionship of marriage. What came her way in the following decades were shadows that lingered, whole seasons of low pressure, and a creeping darkness that would shut both the joyful sun and the romantic moon out of everything but the work.

CHAPTER EIGHT

Madness

Lucy Maud Montgomery's husband, Ewan Macdonald, suffered from repetitive bouts of what was diagnosed as "religious melancholia," a condition no doubt exacerbated by his belief in the doctrine of predestination. This religious concept—which maintained that regardless of your behaviour during the course of your life God had already determined what would become of you after death and wasn't about to change His mind—was an extreme manifestation in an otherwise plain and sensible form of Presbyterianism. In Ewan's case, the belief resulted in a paranoid conviction that he had been born damned and that, as he often declared, God hated him. There was an ebb and flow to his certainty about this, but as time passed the bouts of suffering became longer and longer, often lasting for many months. Not surprisingly, along with this affliction came an overwhelming fear of death, since for Ewan it was the gateway to eternal damnation. There was no way out; no amount of praying or preaching could make any difference. The most he could hope for was as long a life as possible. And after that, the flames of hell forever.

Maud had had some warning that all was not as it should be before she married Ewan in 1911. In 1907, during a long and particularly dismal winter in her grandmother's house, and while Ewan was studying in Glasgow, she confessed to her diary that her own sad feelings were intensified by his letters:

> For the past six weeks Ewan's letters have only made matters worse. He seems dreadfully blue and down hearted. He says he is troubled by headaches and insomnia but he tells me nothing else and I cannot find out what is the cause of this. I cannot help fearing that something serious is the matter with him, for otherwise why should he be so depressed and discouraged. His letters give me the dismal feeling that he is *compelling* himself to write them and has no real interest in writing them—as if his mind and thoughts were exclusively taken up with something else. I didn't realize how much I had been counting on his letters to get me through the winter until they failed me. As it is I really dread getting them,

they worry and depress me so. I have asked him
if he has been to a doctor but he will only say that
doctors cannot help him—nothing more, to all
my questions.

This was the first hint of what, after their marriage,
would become increasingly disturbing information concerning Reverend Ewan Macdonald's mental health; alarming diary entries begin to appear in 1919 and continue over
the next several decades. In the summer of 1919, Ewan
often could not sleep and went out walking on the road in
his nightshirt. He was "very dull at supper time" and "alter-
nated between fits of dull apathy and spells of restless
walking." Pressed, he finally admitted to Maud that "he
was possessed with a horrible dread that he was *eternally
lost*—that there was no hope for him in the next life." This
dread haunted him night and day and he could not banish
it. He was given to staring in a fixed, unblinking way at
nothing in particular and would not speak unless he was
spoken to, and sometimes not even then. He took little
notice of Maud or the children, just "walked the floor
wrapped in his own morbid thoughts." When told he
should consult a specialist, he replied, "I don't want a
doctor—I want a minister," in spite of the fact that he
himself was a minister.

Maud recalled this horrible period in her diary:

> My sufferings mattered nothing to him. His atti-
> tude was 'You do not believe that I am to be
> damned—or that you are—so I do not see why
> you should worry.' I was absolutely alone in my
> despair. I was never in my life so wretchedly
> unhappy as I was in those awful days when
> I went about trying to work and plan and smile
> with that fear that was not to be mentioned
> hanging over me.

Ewan agreed to go to a town named, ironically, Braintree, Massachusetts, to visit his sister Flora. While there he could consult a Boston nerve specialist without the risk of being seen by a parishioner or acquaintance of his famous wife. A week after his departure, Maud received a telegram from Flora telling her that Ewan was no better and that she should come to Massachusetts as soon as possible.

Maud panicked, writing in her journal:

> If Ewan had gone out of his mind completely, what
> was I to do? I had no one in the world to go to for
> help—neither father nor mother nor sister nor
> brother. If this horrible thing had happened—and
> I fully believed it had—the only thing to be done

was to put Ewan in some good sanatorium and go
back to the children. Our home would have to be
broken up and we must go—where?

The reference to the broken home and to her own orphan-
hood does much to illustrate Montgomery's seemingly irra-
tional sense of helpless dependence on her husband. By now
she had published one collection of poetry and eight works
of bestselling fiction. Her name was a household word
throughout much of the English-speaking world, and her
work had already been translated into six foreign languages
and was about to be translated into several more. She had
established a steady and financially rewarding habit of writing, which showed no signs of slowing down, and she could
have taken the children and set up housekeeping anywhere she liked—perhaps in the city, where she might have
assumed her place in a community of the arts. Moreover,
thanks to the work of such liberal thinkers as Nellie
McClung and Agnes Macphail, to mention just two, feminism had started to make its voice heard in Canada. Yet
none of this seems to have entered Maud's mind at that
crucial moment. She must have feared that her status in a
conservative society would be threatened by Ewan's illness,
and that divorce, or even separation, would result in public
humiliation and a disenfranchisement from the very world

she feared, all through her childhood, would exclude her. She craved, and had always craved, safe inclusion in a stable society. Unstable though her marriage may have been, the alternative was unthinkable for someone as insecure as Maud could often be.

Why, then, be so frank about Ewan's disturbing condition in a diary she must have known would eventually be published? There was the catharsis, of course, connected to "writing it all out," and perhaps the comforting sense that in the distant future the blame for her own weaknesses might rest on the shoulders of her husband. But more important, one suspects, is the fact that presenting family secrets to posterity, when one is not around to suffer the consequences, is a very different thing from revealing them in the course of daily life—especially when that daily life revolves around a church and its parishioners.

There is, however, no mistaking her anguish in the face of Ewan's debilitation. She made several entries in her diaries about the "raw state of her nerves" and began to take the narcotic Veronal in order to sleep, though she was aware of its addictive property. While the couple remained in Massachusetts, a terrible heat wave engulfed the state and temperatures rose above one hundred degrees Fahrenheit. For this anxiety-ridden woman and her delusional husband, the heat made sleep even more difficult, and Montgomery began to feel that she herself might completely break down.

They made one or two tortured journeys into Boston to consult an oculist (Ewan had chronic problems with his eyes) and to visit two nerve specialists. The first, a Dr. Garrick, told Maud not to argue with Ewan concerning his phobia about death, which might, he said, be "simple melancholia," then went on to warn her that the problem could be "manic-depressive insanity," adding that she must never let Ewan out of her sight. This suggestion that Ewan might commit suicide terrified her. The second, Dr. Coriat, whom Maud did not like—"His personality did not appeal to me"—said that there was every chance that Ewan could be "quite well" by fall.

In fact, after their return to Leaskdale, that is what appeared to have happened. By September 21 Maud was able to report in her diary that "Ewan is—or seems to be—*absolutely well.*" The italics are rightly placed in this instance, for there had been pure misery right up to the moment of his recovery. But even after he was apparently well, and order had been re-established in their home, Ewan was "haunted by convictions of eternal damnation." Maud reported in her journal that "Ewan had to take two doses of the chloral" on the evening of November 18, and in January 1920 Maud confided that "Ewan was very miserable all day and especially so this afternoon, restless and gloomy. He hasn't had such a bad attack for a long time." The following year, when interviewed by a reporter from *Maclean's* magazine, she talked "brightly and amusingly—and watched Ewan out of the corner of my eye." "That is my existence now," she added. She was living as if there were no relation whatsoever between her inner feelings and her outward deportment.

She had learned early in life how to separate herself from her emotions and behave in a pleasing manner, and often her outer behaviour was at odds with her thoughts and feelings. During the year she lived with her father in Saskatchewan, for example, her true feelings regarding the second Mrs. Montgomery would likely not have been apparent to a bystander—or even another member of the family. Undoubtedly, she completed her chores with a reasonable amount of good humour before going upstairs and writing in her journal that her stepmother was "sulky, jealous, underhanded and *mean*." Later, between 1902 and 1911, when looking after her grandmother, a similar disconnection took place between the dutiful and probably affectionate granddaughter and the way she described the old lady in the pages of her journal. An even odder separation occurred, as we have seen, when she fell passionately in love with Herman Leard and did everything she could to talk herself out of this love. And finally there was her habit of transforming the events of her life, and the feelings those events engendered, into the versions that appeared in her fiction—as well as, one suspects, into the version she presented as fact in her diaries.

EWAN'S NEXT FULL-BLOWN ATTACK did not take place until 1934, although there were episodes—mostly concerning hypochondria—in 1924 and 1927. On May 5, 1934, Maud wrote in her diary: "*What* would I do if Ewan were going to have another serious attack? I could not take him away as I did in 1919—so many reasons make it impossible—and Norval would not be the patient congregation Leaskdale was. Nor would it be easy to hide Ewan's condition here." She reported that all his phobias had manifested themselves again and that he was taking Veronal in order to sleep. He had dreadful headaches and was plagued both by nightmares and wide-awake terrors.

By June he was lying on the bed, groaning and raving about dying—"only a few days more"—and going to hell. Soon he was not only groaning, but grovelling as well, "actually groveling," Montgomery wrote. By June 29 Maud was filling out the necessary forms to have Ewan admitted to Homewood Sanatorium in Guelph, where he was to remain, alternating between signs of recovery and relapse, for almost two months.

While Ewan was in Homewood, Maud was undergoing great difficulties herself, most often associated with sleeplessness. She mentions sleep, or rather the lack of it, literally hundreds of times in her diary and details the drugs she took to help her achieve a full night's rest: Veronal, chloral, bromides, sleeping tablets. Moreover, she was afflicted with asthma attacks, which seemed to happen only at night. She suggested that she, too, might collapse into mental illness. "What would become of us all if I did?" she wrote. She had "a nasty feeling" in her head that had troubled her "off and on for two years now." She had "predictive" dreams that, to her mind, portended bad times ahead. And all the while she was working on the sequel to the life-enhancing and charming *Pat of Silver Bush*, the story of a child who loves her home and its inhabitants so much she cannot bear the idea that any change will come to it or them. On some days Montgomery found it almost impossible to work. On others, in spite of her anxiety, she was pleasantly surprised by the entire chapter she had been able to produce.

After Ewan returned from the sanatorium at the end of the summer, he seemed for a while almost well. In fact he would never fully recover, and perhaps by association, perhaps as a result of her own neurosis, neither would Maud. Six months later, in 1935, she would write in her diary: "Dread! Dread! I eat and drink dread—I lie down with it at night and rise up with it in the morning. It is the constant Dweller on my Threshold." And yet nine days later, on January 24, she announced to her diary that her latest novel, *Mistress Pat*, had arrived at the publishers and they had sent "a nice letter" in reply, telling her they were "delighted with the new Pat."

Less than three weeks later, on February 13, Ewan was dismissed as pastor of the Norval Presbyterian church. The reason, he was informed, was that "people were not coming to church because of him."

Under the circumstances, the defences and denials with which Maud responds to this in her diary are almost impossible to take seriously. If we are to take her at her word, she believed that some of the church elders had been irrationally rude while others had "sat in silence and allowed their Pastor to be insulted." In short, she suggests that there was no real justification for the termination of his appointment. Her old clannish pride seems to have risen up to protect both herself and her husband. She named as a culprit the recent union of the Presbyterian and Methodist churches (Ewan Macdonald had fought against this), as well as the sin of malice on the part of the congregation. Never once did Maud suggest that Ewan's mental illness might have been the cause.

Once again she was grieving at the thought of another abandoned hearth and the spectre of homelessness.

> To leave Norval with its pines—its river—its hills! To leave the beautiful commodious old manse— the lovely tree shaded grounds—my garden—the church I had loved and worked for. This was the bitterest drop in a very bitter cup. And to be torn away from them in such a cruel fashion, not knowing where we could go or what sort of home we could get added to the bitterness of it. I often wonder why I was born to love places so deeply and passionately when my whole life was to be a continual tearing up and uprooting.

And yet the following month a home was found in a new subdivision in the suburb of Swansea, on the western edge of Toronto. It was on Riverside Drive, a long street following the edge of the Humber River Valley. The handsome house, of a mock-Tudor design, was quite unlike anything we associate with Montgomery or her work, but Maud was very pleased with it, and used the word *darling* several times to describe its features. Here, with the wooded ravine behind the property, she could remain close to the natural world she loved so dearly and at the same time enjoy the modern conveniences that such a house would furnish. And although she was to call it Journey's End, the new house filled her with hope. "I *knew* I was going to buy that house," she writes, "— that it had been built for me. My dream had come true . . ."

After such a cheerful announcement, her unfinished sentence at the end of this entry seems to indicate uncertainty— hardly surprising when we consider the horrors of the preceding years—and indeed her troubles were far from over. The family moved to Riverside Drive in April 1935. One year later, on May 3, 1936, Maud was writing in her diary that "Ewan did not sleep at all last night and was very dull and restless all day. This is his worst attack since we came to Toronto." By May 11 he appeared to be well again, but on July 5, their silver wedding anniversary, which Ewan forgot, Maud admitted that the marriage had been for the most part "a nightmare, owing mainly to Ewan's attacks of melancholia." From then on, until the end of the 1930s when she abruptly stopped writing in her journals, Maud would make repeated reference to Ewan's mental, as well as his mostly imagined physical, problems. He is "very dull" (meaning depressed and silent), he wakes her early in the morning "groaning and sighing in distress of mind," and in June 1937 she writes, "Ewan was very poorly today. Refused to eat and took a notion that he couldn't walk. This is his worst attack since the summer of 1934." Then came four unbearably hideous days.

Ewan had been asked if he would preach at the seventy-fifth anniversary of the church in Leaskdale, where he had served as minister from 1909 to 1926, and in spite of his anxiety and Maud's, and several losses of nerve and sleepless nights, on June 26 the couple began the drive to their old home. Several times on the way there, Ewan, confused about the exact location of the house where they were to have supper, became lost. Once they arrived, he contributed little to the conversation and his hands shook so much at dinner that he spilled his tea. They spent the night in the old manse, which would have been filled with the ghosts of the past, and the next day at the church, ignoring Maud's pleas that he should read a sermon, Ewan spoke extemporaneously at both the morning and the evening service. The result, according to Maud, was a humiliating fiasco.

> He tried to speak as usual, got lost almost at once, and after ten minutes of faltering disconnected remarks sat down. I did not know what was coming on Ewan—and in addition there was the

horrible humiliation of seeing my husband make
such a mess of the anniversary service. I don't know
how I kept calm and talked to people afterwards.

But the scenes in the church were not the worst of it.
When they left Leaskdale to return to Toronto after the
evening service and a supper with friends, it was apparent
that Ewan was in a very bad way indeed. He became lost
almost immediately and by constantly veering to the right
managed to put the car in the ditch not once but twice. Back
on the highway after the second upset, they were engulfed in
fog and had to wait on the side of the road until daylight.
When they were able to travel once more, Ewan, no doubt
completely exhausted by now, was again confused about his
surroundings. And then, when they were finally on the
utterly familiar Yonge Street, Ewan stopped the car, leapt
out, and began "marching up and down, talking angrily to
himself." He returned to the vehicle and they set off again,
but still he "talked and raved continually," and by the time
they finally pulled into the driveway on Riverside Drive, it
was 6 A.M.

Maud was beside herself, but not so beside herself
that she neglected to make a record of what transpired.
During the next several weeks, Ewan continued to groan.
He clawed at his head. He had trouble dressing himself. He

had to take "the luminal" in order to sleep. His hands were hot. His pulse was weak. His insides were "boiling." He heard "voices in his ears." It is at this point that we see, in addition to Maud's concern for her husband, something else creeping into the narrative as she herself begins to enter a period of what looks like clinical depression. On June 30 she wrote in her journal:

> I have been out in my garden and enjoyed it a little but oh, I am so tired and lonely and wretched. Ewan's condition is only one of my worries and the lesser. *Everything* seems wrong—nothing seems right. I feel as if I must have failed terribly somewhere—but where? I have tried to do the best I could by my husband and boys. I don't think I ever neglected them.

While, on various occasions, both boys had given Maud reason to worry, it is also true that hers was a nature that could turn a failed exam into a national emergency, and this could only have made the boys themselves more anxious and therefore more difficult. That being said, they appeared to have been affectionate, polite, and well behaved even if, as they grew into manhood, they did not meet their mother's expectations in other ways. And what could it have been like to grow up in a house with a preternaturally high-strung mother on the one hand and a despondent and at times delusional father on the other? Nothing that these boys did could have justified Montgomery's referring to her son Hugh, who died in infancy, as the only "son who has never hurt me or disappointed me." We can only be grateful that this sentiment was confessed to her diary and, as far as we know, never spoken aloud.

It is important to remember that not only are we presented with only one point of view (Maud's) in the diaries, but that this point of view is expressed in a form that most consistently records the lows of her existence interspersed with a very few highs and almost no neutrals. Maud admitted that she used the journal to "write things out," and to get off her chest emotions that in common discourse would be unmentionable. Hence we hear only about Ewan's sessions of melancholia and little about the comparatively calm seasons in between, or the grown-up boys' various disasters with women and their educational and career failures with little mention of their equally plentiful successes. Moreover, as her biographer Mary Rubio has pointed out, the diaries were edited and rewritten by Maud herself, often from notes taken in haste, then worked up into a particular kind of narrative later.

As the years passed, however, whenever Maud wrote in her diary, she was almost always in a state of alarm, verging on panic and despair. Observations about the beauty of the perceived world and the joy connected to writing appear less and less often as the years go by, and when they do appear they are frequently elegiac. She remembers with sadness the landscape of her girlhood in Prince Edward Island, and she recalls the excitement she used to feel when presented with a copy of a new book, an excitement she is unable to muster by the time she is middle-aged. Her legal problems with her first publisher and a lawsuit brought against Ewan as the result of a car accident take up a considerable amount of space, and there are times when Lucy Maud's previously lyrical world becomes bleakly prosaic.

In and around 1937, as the diary shifts away from descriptions of Ewan's mental state and begins to describe her own despondency, it is difficult to believe that the sorrows and anxieties being detailed are not ones that continually surround her. Over and over again we hear about her suffering. She is "intently worn out" and "too tired to care for anything." She did "spade work" for the current novel "but felt very tired and listless." "*Everything*," she writes, "is poisoned by the awful situation I am in." "All my days seem ghastly now," she confesses a few months later, "but regularly every few weeks comes one that stands out in its ghastliness." How disheartening it is to compare such lines with passages written in 1889 when she was only fourteen. Not yet self-consciously a writer but obviously brimming with talent, she was able to use her child's eye and her great ability to bring a simple potato field to life:

> We were picking potatoes all day up in our hill field. I don't think anybody ever got to such a pitch of virtue as to like potato-picking. I hate it! But since pick I had to I was glad I was up in that hill field because I love that field. There is such a glorious view from it—the deep blue sea, the pond as blue as sapphire, the groves of maple and birch just turning to scarlet and gold. I just love to look at such things.

And then, filled with youth and enthusiasm, she adds, "To be sure, potato-picking has its funny side. It would have made a hermit laugh to see Lu and me as we trudged home tonight, in tattered, beclayed old dresses, nondescript hats and faces plastered with dirt and mud."

There is evidence of this sense of humour even during the bleak years of her maturity. It is there in the novels, of course, but also in her public appearances. At a speech delivered to eight hundred women in the Forrester's Hall in Toronto in

October 1913, for example, a city journalist was impressed both by Montgomery's wit and charm and by the reaction of the members of her audience, who "smiled and laughed and applauded and to all intents and purposes were girls again in their old homes." And following a talk at a Guelph, Ontario, women's club in early 1927, the local paper reported that Lucy Maud Montgomery "proved to be one of the most entertaining speakers ever heard locally," citing as particularly memorable her "brilliant wit" and "sly humour." Even as late as 1937, a Beaverton, Ontario, newspaper described a lecture she had given in that town as "interesting" and "humorous."

But by 1938 there was little or no humour left in Maud. In a frightening and apparently unconscious echo of her husband's words, she reported, "It is not my body that is sick—but my soul." Later that year and into 1939 things appeared to take a brighter turn. Maud admitted to feeling better, the boys seemed to be doing fairly well, and even Ewan's chronic hypochondria did not seem to devastate her as it did in the past. And then, abruptly, at the end of June 1939, after fifty years of examined life, the diaries cease. Only two short entries come after.

The first, from July 8, 1941, reads, "O God, such an end to life. Such suffering and wretchedness." The second, from March 23, 1942, is even more disturbing: "Since then my life has been hell, hell, hell. My mind has gone—everything in the world I lived for has gone—the world has gone mad. I shall be driven to end my life. O God forgive me. Nobody dreams what my awful position is." Lucy Maud Montgomery died a month later, on April 24, 1942. She was sixty-seven years old.

CHAPTER NINE

Sleep

All through her adult life Lucy Maud Montgomery would struggle with sleep, achieving it, and then losing it, over and over until it became an obsession. Day after day, walking the floors of one house or another, she would imagine sleep as if she were having an unrequited love affair with unconsciousness. She would curse sleep and coax sleep, but like any ambivalent lover, the more she courted it, the further it withdrew. Insomnia quickly became the route to fully conscious darkness and dread.

Sleep, when it did arrive, was no escape; the beloved slumber could, at times, imprison her in an unwholesome embrace, introducing her to its ugly stepsibling, nightmare.

Her nightmares were many and various. She dreamt of finding coffins placed at the end of her bed, pinning down her feet; her husband hanging, alive, from the end of a rope; previously unknown rooms in one manse or another, or these houses in flames. She dreamt of girls with hair the colour of fire emerging from the furniture of her bedroom.

She dreamt of a high white board "like a tombstone" with the words *Paid! Paid! Paid!* painted on it in large black letters. She dreamt of sitting down to dine in the kitchen of the old house and noted in her diary that "at that gruesome supper table, three of the party were *dead*!"

She believed that her nightmares were predictive, and often it seemed as if this were indeed the case. But there was another side to her questionable gift of second sight. She quite literally looked at everything, nightmares included, at least twice. Once when the event or dream was happening, again while she determined its significance, sometimes a third time when she recorded it in her diary, and occasionally once more, when she refashioned it to be used in fiction. This combination of dream, memory, reflection, and transformation—and the way she entered her unconscious through imagination and at the same time paid attention to both symbols and mythology—was in full force in her psyche well before Carl Jung's groundbreaking publications concerning the unconscious could have been known to her. But one cannot help but wonder what Jung himself would have made of Montgomery, her personality, her writing, and her desire to mythologize her surroundings. As it was, this multi-layered response to daily life must have been exhausting and may itself have contributed to her inability to sleep.

Quite early on, she had begun to fear the night as a place of sleeplessness, of waking dreams, and of nightmares. In spite of countless romantic references to moonlight and starlight in her fiction, and to rooms warmly lit by lamplight and by candlelight, it was shadow, not radiance, that most often claimed her once the sun had set. Her seeming addiction to detailing sunsets and twilights in her writing, if it sprang from anything at all beyond poetic convention, may have come from a desire to hold on to the fading light. After the sunset came total wide-awake darkness. At a time when the night was far less brightly lit than it is today, that darkness, and the terrors it brought to her, would have been absolute: her only escape from it would have been sleep. Almost as soon as she was independent enough to do so, she began, with the help of prescriptions written by several doctors, to self-medicate.

A dizzying array of drugs is catalogued in her diaries—bromides, Veronal, Nembutal, chloral, Medinal, Luminal—and it is frightening to note how, in the indexes of her final two published journals, the list under "Drugs and Medications" grows in length. Occasionally, when things were very, very bad, she would drug herself during the day. But most often these medications were part of her nightly quest for sleep. Many times she would be joined in this search by her angst-ridden husband who was struggling with his own horrors. The anguish of this insomnia-dominated marriage is painful even to think about, and must have been almost impossible to endure.

Later in her life, her sleeplessness had less to do with her fears concerning the mental state of her husband and became attached instead to her anxiety concerning her son Chester, who had married against her will and who, after fathering a child in this marriage, went on to have a surprisingly indiscreet affair with another woman before returning briefly to his wife and producing another child. (I use the word *surprisingly* because his mother clearly knew all about the affair, as she did about almost every facet of his life, good and bad.) Chester was on various occasions found in compromising situations with women, was dismissed from universities and colleges, and was fired from jobs, each unpleasant episode causing his mother more and more anguish. Montgomery did not live long enough to see what finally became of Chester, but her predictions that he would come to a sorry end were accurate to a fault. Although he finally became a lawyer, he would open and close practices with alarming frequency and eventually, while working for the government, was convicted of and imprisoned for embezzlement.

Her younger son, Stuart, would also disappoint now and then, though his misdemeanours pale in comparison to Chester's. On several occasions Montgomery was brought to the edge of reason—almost to hysteria—by worry over Stuart's exams, and at one point she was driven to what looks like nearly full-blown rage when he chose to date a girl she did not approve of. "Joy was certainly no companion for my son," she wrote in her diary, adding cruelly, "The thought that one day he might ask me to accept that bootlegger's spawn as my daughter was something I could not bear." Stuart Macdonald, unlike his brother, led a conventional and successful life, eventually becoming a respected physician and, after marrying Ruth Steele, a devoted family man. But he never fully forgave his mother for her brutal, unfair, and angry remarks concerning his first girlfriend.

Rage and sleep do not make good bedfellows, and it is difficult to believe that Montgomery's anguish was not, at least at times, a variant of rage. Often her intense anger was brought about by the actions of her sons. In spite of her Herculean efforts, she could never hope to have complete power over them, and this lack of control led her into some very dark places. Her ability to walk her own demons into the lives of her sons was not her most attractive attribute. Her controlling personality and her need to manipulate by inflicting guilt must have made for a very complicated childhood and young adulthood for two boys forced to tiptoe around such an extremely volatile mother. For Maud, motherhood was yet another, even more burdensome source of anxiety and frustration, and anxiety and frustration murdered sleep.

Still, it was likely when she was in the grips of insomnia that she became most human: vulnerable, helpless, her unconscious rising to the surface and then sinking again, her thoughts slipping in and out of her grasp. Often she would pace the floor of a dark hallway, her face ravaged by lack of sleep, the voice of her anger stifled in her throat. In nightclothes she would be fragile, unprotected, the persona of the famous author discarded with her dress and stockings like any other kind of costume, fear waging a battle in her mind. It is difficult to believe that, even after a childhood spent secretly scribbling by candlelight, she might have used the night hours for composition, such was the horror of her sleeplessness. Instead, various realities would have assaulted her, and the adult narratives she spun at night were likely those of old and new grievances: her mother's death, her father's absence, her husband's illness, her sons' misdeeds—a familiar litany—and running beneath it all, barely acknowledged by her, the poisonous stream of her own self-hatred.

During the last decades of her life she had found herself living near two ravines gouged out of the landscape by rivers, the Credit in Norval and the Humber in west Toronto. Loving descriptions of both are included in her diaries, but at night, if she thought of them at all, those ravines might have assumed the dark aspect of an underworld, and if so the rivers moving through them grew as inky and as lethal as the Styx. In the last few years of her life, when even the daylight hours brought no comfort, those shady regions may have offered an invitation to a different kind of sleep, one that was easier to achieve. The thought may have entered her mind that, surrounded as she was by bottles of various pills, there was a kind of sleep she could count on. She could, if she chose, descend into the ravine, cross the river, and never again awaken into painful life.

There is no direct evidence that Lucy Maud Montgomery took her own life, but the indirect evidence presents a compelling case. Her daily life during this period, when she kept no journals and spun no fiction, is almost too distressing to imagine. She would have had to grapple with her own anguish, both physical and mental, hour by waking hour with no outlet or relief. Perhaps, as suggested by Mary Rubio in her biography, Maud *was* able at least to record her thoughts—if not create fiction—and that record was destroyed, possibly by her son Chester. Or perhaps the medication she must have been using constantly by then dropped a curtain between her and her torment. Maybe she really did die of natural causes: coronary thrombosis being the primary cause given on her death certificate. Whatever the case, in the end, on that final day in April, sleep, whether chosen by her or granted to her, would have been welcome. One fervently hopes that, when it arrived, it held her in a warm and comforting embrace. She had been waiting for it, praying for it, almost all her life.

CHAPTER TEN

Her Reader

Early on a Friday afternoon in the long ago twenties of what is now a former century, a girl of eleven walks up the lane that runs from her Ontario farmhouse to the road. She is heading for the village two miles away. I think it is likely August and therefore hot, but she is wearing a pinafore over a three-quarter-sleeved cotton dress to protect it from being soiled after a day spent mostly out of doors. She is bareheaded—there being no notion at this time that the sun is something to be shunned—and her skin is summer brown. She reaches one hand up now and then to touch her dark, recently bobbed hair, while the other keeps a firm grasp on the handle of her brother's red wagon. Which brother the wagon belongs to is anyone's guess; there are already several—all younger than she—so perhaps it is considered communal family property. But one thing is certain in these gender-specific days: the wagon does not belong to her. What she is after in the village does not belong to her either, but more about that later.

It is important for us to know what she sees as she walks to her destination along the gravel road, because after her summer's reading it has become important for her to know. Mr. Moore, who owns the farm across the road, is plowing the field adjacent to his home, and the girl looks at the details of his flower garden and clapboard house, even one of the sheds out back, the curve of its sagging roof. She knows the names of the two workhorses pulling the plow, just as she knows the names of the horses on her own farm, and of those on all the farms in the district, for agricultural animals are still given names and the quirks of their personalities are much discussed. She also knows the physical characteristics of the field and especially of the creek that runs through it. The creek runs under the road on its way to her father's property, where it disappears into dim, mysterious cedar woods after crossing a damp pasture. The girl and her brothers have constructed forts and playhouses in the woods and have either pushed each other or waded voluntarily into the creek. Now, as a result of a summer spent reading, these memories seem to have taken on an episodic importance in a way they never have before, and she senses she might find a use for them in the future. She also wants to name the woods in which the small dramas took place, wants to call it something like the Haunted Forest, but knows that a name such as that doesn't fit the ways in which she and her brothers have passed their time there.

To follow the contours of his gently rising land, Mr. Moore is plowing east to west, rather than north to south, and he is presented to the girl in profile, almost silhouetted against the hills that dominate Percy Township in Northumberland County, Ontario. The girl has been told that the hills, which gather height and dimension as they approach the nearby village, and then the great lake ten miles farther on, were the shores of that lake in a time so long in the past that no one is quite sure whether it was thousands or millions or billions of years ago. But such vast acreages of time seem no more incomprehensible to her than the notion that the place where her own village stands was a wilderness only two hundred years before, not the familiar cluster of buildings that represents all she understands of community.

To her, this summer, her small community has become almost mythical. She will never forget her shock of recognition after opening a brownish-green book with a lovely young woman's profile on the cover. She had been hesitant to read it until her mother, who had bought the book a decade before when it was first published, assured her that it was about a girl her age. And once the girl in Ontario had followed Anne Shirley home to Green Gables, and had begun to know the people in Avonlea, Prince Edward Island, she realized she could just as easily have been reading about her own world. She had never had an experience like that before. Until then, the books she read were about children and animals in faraway England. The Anne books and the Emily books have electrified her own small life, added meaning and intensity even to the most ordinary of its attributes. The neighbours, the fields, the special chosen places in the landscape, the prankster boys, the politics she hears her father complain about before he goes to the town hall in the village are important to her now in ways they never were before.

Soon she is passing her uncle's farm, so called because he is the one who performs all the physical labour there. In truth, the land and everything on it belongs to the girl's maternal grandmother, who has always been hard-willed and who, by this time, is beginning to lose her eyesight, which seems to make her tighten her grip on the property. This particular uncle is engaged to be married, and has been for some time, but is unable to set a date for the wedding because he cannot imagine leaving his mother.

As the girl passes the farm, a farm not nearly as wooded or well watered as her own, she thinks about the ring her uncle has given to the young woman; white gold with two amethysts set on either side of a small sharp diamond. Jewellery this glamorous and costly is seldom seen, and the ring was much admired by the girl when, a few years before, her uncle opened the small velvet box to show it to his family. She thinks, also, of the "lost diamond," an ancestral legend in the family of Emily Starr, from *Emily of New Moon*, and how Emily finds it eventually, as the girl always knew she would. There are legends like this in her own family, tales filled with portents, and separated lovers, and early death. She has always been fascinated by such stories, but now, after spending July with *Anne of Green Gables* and August with *Emily of New Moon*, these family tales have gained an added dimension.

The west field of her uncle's farm abuts the graveyard, which lies, like a miniature medieval city, on the very edge of the village. It is a picturesque acre, gently rolling, punctuated here and there with ten or twelve impressive granite pillars, but mostly filled, in an orderly way, with marble headstones on which clasped hands, weeping willows, and occasionally birds in flight are carved. No one in the community is wealthy enough to afford an angel in memory of a loved one. Even if they were, the money would likely have gone toward building the war memorial that stands down the road a little closer to town. It is a modest example of its kind, though on its surface it is possible to find names from almost every family in the vicinity. The girl barely remembers the war, being still quite small when it ended, but now, having begun her introduction to Anne's daughter in *Rilla of Ingleside*, she believes that she does remember it, has lived through it. And although no one in her own family was directly affected, she believes she understands with greater clarity the losses it brought about. The war is still much talked about by the master at school and is the subject of many of the poems that she and her classmates are required to memorize and recite in unison. In those poems there are references to the Mother Country of England, whose call was answered by her sons here in the Dominion of Canada. Because of her summer reading, the girl knows more about the emotions connected to this war, about those boys who departed, and about the trance of grief that existed, and exists even now.

In the graveyard, over the plots of their pioneer ancestors, the girl has often sworn eternal friendship with other girls of roughly her age, this being considered a very solemn and romantic thing to do. It seems that after all the labour of clearing land, removing stumps and boulders, building log houses and rail fences, and somewhat later brick or frame houses and barns, a general decision had been taken never to move elsewhere, for any one of the girl's classmates was able to find ancestral graves over which to cement a friendship, if the occasion demanded that they do so. And with those ancestral graves came the ancestral stories of families other than her own, stories that the girl now believes to be charged with meaning, in the same way that the stories she has recently read are resonant and haunting. The landscape surrounding the graveyard has become more powerful as well. The girl thinks about how the roads, hills, rivers, and sometimes even villages bear the names of the settlers who are buried in this spot. And she knows that Anne or Emily would likely have sworn eternal friendship over graves in their own landscapes near hills and roads named after their own ancestors.

The village the girl is now entering is called Castleton, a name relating neither to a settler family nor a castle but connected instead to some lost place in the Mother Country that one or two of the first settlers must have hoped to keep bright in their memories. Now, however, only a century or so later, this humble place is substantial enough that the hamlet that inspired its name is never thought of, and most of the newer Castleton's inhabitants would be surprised to learn that another Castleton existed anywhere else on the planet.

Essentially, with a few straggling exceptions, the village is built around a junction formed by two roads: the one on which the girl's father's farm is situated and the one that enters the village from the north and heads toward the great lake. Having walked by the twenty or so houses on the first road, the girl is now approaching the buildings that make up the central core: two general stores, a hardware store, the small, brick town hall, and the frame hotel that also houses a very small branch of the Standard Bank of Canada. Drama, the child now knows, drama of a very significant, almost Shakespearean nature, could be unfolding in the rooms of any one of these structures. Because of her summer reading she has become enlightened to the fact that stories unfolding in the plain brick and clapboard houses of the Dominion of Canada can be just as riveting as those that take place in large, dark country houses set in sad, neglected grounds near glens and moors.

What she has come for is housed in the bank. So great is her desire, she has once or twice fantasized about committing an act of robbery but eventually decided that a more conventional method could be used. She leaves her wagon on the wooden sidewalk, walks up the steps, and opens the door. Mr. Morton, the bank manager (who is also the teller and the secretary), is standing behind the counter. There are no customers, which pleases the girl because she knows that what she wants to do will seem foolish to adults and, this being the case, the fewer of these around the better.

Mr. Morton is relatively new to town, having arrived from Belleville the previous year to take the place of the retiring Mr. Dempsey. Several romantic rumours have already begun to circulate about this young, good-looking man, and after her summer reading, these rumours make the girl believe there is gold, of a sort, in simple gossip. But all these possible narratives pale in comparison to what it is that Mr. Morton has in his possession. The child stares at the young man until he finally looks up from the column of sums that occupies him.

"What is it, Marian?" he asks in a surprisingly respectful manner. He has likely taken into consideration that her father is reeve of the township.

Just the previous week, the girl has finished the last page of *Emily's Quest*, the third volume in the Emily trilogy by Lucy Maud Montgomery. She is bursting with the idea of climbing the Alpine Path of publishing, first in seed catalogues and then, later, with a big American publisher in Boston or New York.

"I want to borrow your typewriter for the weekend," she says. She knows there is not one other machine of this nature for at least ten miles.

Mr. Morton is struck dumb.

"You won't need it till Monday," the girl continues, "and I promise to take care of it. I won't let the boys anywhere near it."

"What on earth," Mr. Morton asks with a vaguely condescending smile, "would you be wanting to do with a typewriter?"

The girl is surprised. Either he really doesn't know or he's pretending not to know.

"I am going to write a novel," she says.

ASTONISHINGLY, the bank manager in Castleton, Ontario, permitted my mother to take the typewriter back with her to the farm all those years ago. He carried it out of the bank, placed it in the wagon, and after making her promise to have it back first thing on Monday morning he wished her luck with the novel.

Although my mother discovered to her great frustration that she knew nothing about typewriters and the bizarre scrambling of the alphabet in the placement of their keys, and therefore did not complete the first chapter of her novel, she kept the intense love of reading—and of reading Canadian authors—that had been born in her that summer. And decades after she returned the typewriter to Mr. Morton at the Standard Bank in Castleton, she passed on those books by Lucy Maud Montgomery, and that love of reading Canadian authors, to me.

SOURCES

Because of the many gifted and dedicated scholars, researchers, and writers who have been drawn to this subject, reading about the life of Lucy Maud Montgomery is an engaging and rewarding experience. Among the numerous books that were available to me, and which I read over the past two or three years, I would like to call attention to those I found to be particularly helpful.

Foremost, of course, were the five published volumes of Montgomery's diaries (*The Selected Journals of L.M. Montgomery*, Vols. I to V, Toronto: Oxford University Press Canada, 1983, 1985, 1987, 1998, 2004), painstakingly edited and annotated by celebrated Montgomery scholars Mary Rubio and Elizabeth Waterston. Added to the diaries were two books recently published by these same scholars: Mary Rubio's groundbreaking biography *Lucy Maud Montgomery: The Gift of Wings* (Toronto: Doubleday Canada, 2008) and Elizabeth Waterston's fascinating examination of Montgomery's creative process, *Magic Island: The Fictions of L.M. Montgomery* (Toronto: Oxford University Press Canada, 2008).

I read and greatly enjoyed *Looking for Anne: How Lucy Maud Montgomery Dreamed Up a Literary Classic* (Toronto: Key Porter Books, 2008) by Irene Gammel, who has also published the edifying *Making Avonlea: L.M. Montgomery and Popular Culture* (Toronto: University of Toronto Press, 2002). *Before Green Gables* (Toronto: Penguin Canada, 2008), Budge Wilson's prequel to *Anne of Green Gables*, was not only convincing but also very informative.

Much wonderful work on Montgomery has been undertaken by Prince Edward Island scholar Elizabeth Rollins Epperly. Two of her books I found indispensable: *Through Lover's Lane: L.M. Montgomery's Photography and Visual Imagination* (Toronto: University of Toronto Press, 2007) and *Imagining Anne: The Island Scrapbooks of Lucy Maud Montgomery* (Toronto: Penguin Canada, 2008). I would also like to thank Betsy Epperly for showing me the scrapbooks some years ago when I was in Prince Edward Island.

An earlier book, *The Wheel of Things: A Biography of L.M. Montgomery, Author of Anne of Green Gables* (Toronto: Fitzhenry & Whiteside, 1975) by Mollie Gillen, was enlightening when it came to biographical details, as was Montgomery's autobiography, *The Alpine Path: The Story of My Career* (Toronto: Fitzhenry & Whiteside, 1917).

To gain a better understanding of Montgomery's influence on subsequent generations of Canadian writers, I read the afterwords to three of the Montgomery titles currently published in McClelland & Stewart's New Canadian Library series, and I myself wrote the fourth. Margaret Atwood furnished the afterword for *Anne of Green Gables* (Toronto: M&S, 1992), Alice Munro wrote about *Emily of New Moon* (M&S, 1989), I dealt with *Emily Climbs* (M&S, 1989), and poet P.K. Page responded to *Emily's Quest* (M&S, 1989).

And of course it is no good reading these afterwords without reading that which precedes them. Perhaps the greatest delight for me was the rereading of Montgomery herself. Anyone wanting to know about this author should, in my opinion, give themselves over to the true pleasure of reading her complete works.

Finally, I would like to thank the staff of the Archival and Special Collections of the University of Guelph Library, who on several occasions over the last three years allowed me access to the L.M. Montgomery Collection. Their help is deeply appreciated.

ACKNOWLEDGMENTS

During the time when I was thinking about, reading about, and finally writing about Lucy Maud Montgomery, I had many conversations with a number of people concerning Montgomery and how her work had affected them. I am particularly grateful to Alice Munro, Joan Clark, Michael Phillips, Jim Polk, Stan Dragland, Anne Hart, David Staines, Anne Michaels, Dorota Filipczak (in Poland), and Connie Rooke for their insight and especially for their encouragement.

Finally, I would like to thank senior editor Alex Schultz for his perceptive and sensitive work on the text, and, as always, Heather Sangster for her meticulous attention to detail.

1874   Lucy Maud Montgomery is born in Clifton, Prince Edward Island, to Hugh John Montgomery and Clara Macneill.

1875   Clara Macneill-Montgomery, mother of two-year-old Lucy Maud, dies. The infant child will be raised by her maternal grandparents rather than her father.

1889   A fourteen-year-old Lucy Maud begins what she calls "a new kind of diary." She will keep journals of this nature for the rest of her life.

1890   Montgomery and her grandfather Senator Donald Montgomery make a journey by train to Prince Albert, Saskatchewan, so that Maud may spend a year with her father. Before leaving Charlottetown, they meet Prime Minister John A. Macdonald, who is visiting Prince Edward Island. During this year she experiences the first of what would become many newspaper publications of her work.

1893–94   Montgomery attends Prince of Wales College in Charlottetown and obtains a teaching certificate. She teaches for one year.

1895–96   She attends Dalhousie University and continues to publish in newspapers and magazines.

1896–98   Unable to afford another year at university, she teaches school in Belmont, Prince Edward Island. She accepts Edwin Simpson's proposal of marriage and, in 1898, while teaching in Lower Bedeque, Prince Edward Island, falls in love with Herman Leard.

1898–1900   After her grandfather's death, Montgomery returns to Cavendish to be with her grandmother.

1901   She accepts a position with the *Halifax Daily Echo*.

1902   She returns to Cavendish and her grandmother.

1905   Lucy Maud Montgomery writes *Anne of Green Gables*. She is being courted by a young Presbyterian minister, Ewan Macdonald.

1906   Ewan proposes before leaving for Scotland for further studies, and Maud accepts. The

	marriage cannot take place until after her grandmother's death.
1907	Montgomery is offered a publishing contract for *Anne of Green Gables* by L.C. Page of Boston.
1908	*Anne of Green Gables* is published and is a great critical and financial success.
1909	*Anne of Avonlea* is published. *Anne of Green Gables* is beginning to be translated and published elsewhere. This will continue as the years pass.
1910	*Kilmeny of the Orchard* is published.
1911	Her grandmother dies; and Lucy Maud Montgomery marries the Reverend Ewan Macdonald. They honeymoon in the British Isles, then move to Leaskdale, Ontario, where Ewan is to be minister.
1912	Her first son, Chester, is born. *Chronicles of Avonlea* is published.
1913	She writes and publishes *The Golden Road*.
1914	Her second son, Hugh, dies soon after his birth. England declares war on Germany and the First World War begins.

1915	Maud and Ewan's third son, Stuart, is born. *Anne of the Island* is published.
1916–18	Legal battles with L.C. Page. Montgomery begins to publish with McClelland, Goodchild & Stewart in Canada and Frederick A. Stokes Company in the United States. The war ends.
1919	Ewan Macdonald has a nervous breakdown. Maud's beloved cousin Frede dies.
1920–23	Legal battles with L.C. Page. *Rilla of Ingleside* is published in 1920. *Emily of New Moon* appears in 1923.
1924	"Church Union" between the Methodist and Presbyterian churches occurs, and Ewan Macdonald and his congregation opt out.
1925	*Emily Climbs* is published.
1926	*The Blue Castle* is published. Ewan becomes minister at Norval and the family moves to this community.
1927	The last of the Emily trilogy, *Emily's Quest,* appears in print.

1928	Lawsuits with L.C. Page are finally resolved in Montgomery's favour.
1929	*Magic for Marigold* is published.
1931	*A Tangled Web* is published.
1933	*Pat of Silver Bush* is published.
1934	Ewan Macdonald is hospitalized in Guelph for problems with mental health.
1935	*Mistress Pat* is published. Ewan, dismissed from the church, moves with Maud to the west side of Toronto. Montgomery is inducted as an Officer into the Order of the British Empire.
1936	The Government of Canada begins to develop a national park in and around Cavendish, Prince Edward Island. *Anne of Windy Poplars* is published.
1937	*Jane of Lantern Hill* is published.
1939	Lucy Maud Montgomery's last book, *Anne of Ingleside*, is published. The Second World War breaks out.
1942	After months and months of anguish, Lucy Maud Montgomery dies on April 24.